LEE ELLIOT MAJOR
AND STEPHEN MACHIN

Social Mobility
And Its Enemies

A PELICAN BOOK

PELICAN
an imprint of
PENGUIN BOOKS

PELICAN BOOKS

UK | USA | Canada | Ireland | Australia
India | New Zealand | South Africa

Penguin Books is part of the Penguin Random House
group of companies whose addresses can be found at
global.penguinrandomhouse.com.

Penguin
Random House
UK

First published 2018
004

Text copyright © Lee Elliot Major and Stephen Machin, 2018

The moral rights of the authors have been asserted

Book design by Matthew Young
Set in 10/14.664 pt FreightText Pro
Typeset by Jouve (UK), Milton Keynes
Printed and bound in Great Britain by Clays Ltd, Elcograf S.p.A.

A CIP catalogue record for this book is available from the British Library

ISBN: 978-0-241-31702-0

MIX
Paper from
responsible sources
FSC® C018179

Penguin Random House is committed to a
sustainable future for our business, our readers
and our planet. This book is made from Forest
Stewardship Council® certified paper.

www.greenpenguin.co.uk

Contents

LIST OF FIGURES   vii

INTRODUCTION
The Tale of the Two Davids   1

PART ONE: SOCIAL MOBILITY AND INEQUALITY

CHAPTER 1
Mobility and Inequality   23

CHAPTER 2
Rising and Falling Economic Tides   43

CHAPTER 3
Mapping Mobility   59

PART TWO: SOCIAL MOBILITY AND EDUCATION

CHAPTER 4
The Ever-Escalating Educational Arms Race   81

CHAPTER 5
Education's Lost Souls   113

CHAPTER 6
Britain's Privately Educated Elites   129

PART THREE: IMPROVING SOCIAL MOBILITY

CHAPTER 7
The Way Ahead   151

CHAPTER 8
Rethinking Work and Education   175
Improving Absolute Mobility

CHAPTER 9
Unlocking the Elites   193
Improving Relative Mobility

NOTES   221

INDEX   255

List of Figures

0.1	Intergenerational Mobility in the 1958 Birth Cohort	6
0.2	Intergenerational Mobility in the 1970 Birth Cohort	7
0.3	90–10 Wage Differentials, 1980 to 2017	9
1.1	International Differences in Intergenerational Elasticity	28
1.2	Probability of Moving from Bottom to Top Quintile	32
1.3	The *Great Gatsby* Curve	36
1.4	Percentage of Owner-Occupiers at Age 42 in Two Generations	40
2.1	Real Wages in the 1980s	48
2.2	Real Wages in the 1990s and 2000s	50
2.3	UK Productivity, 1980–2017	52
2.4	Real Wage Changes, 2008–2017	53
3.1	The Geography of Upward Mobility in America	64

3.2	Social Mobility in England by Local Authority	74
3.3	Leave Voters in the EU Referendum in England	75
3.4	Brexit and Social Mobility in England's 320 Local Authorities	76
4.1	Private Tutoring of Secondary School Children, 2005–2016	85
4.2	Cognitive Development of Young Children and Their Parents' Socio-Economic Status	93
4.3	Highest Educational Qualification: Percentage of 26–30-year-olds	98
4.4	Educational Inequality, 1981 to 2013	99
4.5	Wage Differentials by Highest Education Qualification, 26–30-year-olds	103
5.1	Sample Question in OECD Basic Numeracy Test, 2012	116
5.2	Numeracy Levels by Age: England	118
5.3	Numeracy Levels, 16–29-year-olds, by Country	119
5.4	Numeracy Level 1 or Lower in England, by Age and Parental Education	126
6.1	Percentage in Selected Professions Who Were Privately Educated (2012)	135
6.2	Private/State School Wage Differentials for 33–34-year-olds	143
7.1	Percentage of Dual-University-Graduate Families by Region	167
7.2	Average Family Income by Region	168

The Tale of the Two Davids

David C: 'It's where you going to, not where you're from that counts.'

David B: 'I know that if I set my mind to do something, even if people are saying I can't do it, I will achieve it.'

One David was born in a terraced house in East London, his father a kitchen fitter, his mother a hairdresser. The other David grew up in an idyllic village in the English countryside, his father a stockbroker (and the direct descendant of King William IV), his mother the daughter of a baronet. The first David left school at sixteen without any qualifications; the second studied at Eton and Oxford. One married an Essex girl. The other married the daughter of a wealthy aristocrat.

Both Davids have led successful lives and, in their own way, each highlights Britain's social mobility problem.

David Beckham's meteoric rise is a rare occurrence in modern Britain. Few children born to poor parents climb the income ladder all the way to the stratospheric heights of global stardom. A shockingly high number leave school without the basic literacy and numeracy skills needed to get on in life, and end up in the same poorly paid jobs as their fathers and mothers.

David Cameron continued a tradition that has seen successive generations of social elites retain their grip on the country's most influential positions. Every prime minister since the end of the Second World War who has attended an English university has attended just one institution: Oxford.

And Eton remains the exclusive breeding ground of Britain's future elites. Cameron was berated by his own Education Secretary for surrounding himself at the heart of Government with a 'preposterous' number of fellow Old Etonians.[1]

Social mobility tells us how likely we are to climb up (or fall down) the economic or social ladder of life. And whilst some people are upwardly and downwardly mobile, too many of us are destined to end up on the same rungs occupied by our parents.

The tale of the two Davids can be used to illustrate the different ways of measuring social mobility. Each measure highlights a different way of benchmarking 'success' in life. Beckham's rags-to-riches story is defined by how rich he has become compared with his parents. We call this 'intergenerational income mobility'. Economists like to use income as a metric because it is a reliable way of comparing one generation's status to the next, or of comparing one country's mobility levels to another's. A pound is a pound, and a dollar is a dollar, even if its purchasing power changes over time. They talk in terms of 'intergenerational income persistence', the opposite of mobility: it tells us how the incomes of families persist from one generation to the next.

Sticky Ends: The Deepening U-curve

Figures we have compiled reveal that the low levels of income mobility in Britain are due to a stickiness, or immobility, at the bottom and top of the income spectrum. Children born into the highest-earning families are most likely themselves in later life to be among the highest earners; at the other end of the scale children from the lowest-earning families are likely to mirror their forebears as low-earning adults.

The U-shaped curves in Figures 0.1 and 0.2 show how this stickiness for the richest and poorest in society has increased over recent generations. They are generated using data for children and adults grouped into five earnings categories, from poorest to richest.[2] The first graph charts trends from the National Child Development Study, which follows the lives of people born in Britain in one week in March 1958.[3]

If there was complete mobility, the chart would be a flat line; every bar would be at 20 per cent, reflecting an equal chance of ending up in one of the five quintiles. But there is instead a shallow U-shaped curve. A quarter of the sons from the fifth poorest homes remained in the poorest fifth of incomes as adults. And 32 per cent of children born into the richest top fifth of homes stayed among the richest homes when they grew up.

The second graph reveals a deeper U-shaped curve describing the mobility of the generation born in 1970. Over a third (35 per cent) of the sons born in 1970 from the fifth poorest homes remained in the poorest fifth of incomes as adults. Meanwhile 41 per cent of children born into the richest top fifth of homes stayed among the richest homes as adults. In just one decade, Britain had become less mobile.

Beckham is the exception to the rule – in a generation of lower social mobility. His annual earnings make him one of the most mobile people in Britain.[4] He is paid millions of pounds, hundreds of times more than the money made by his father. Born in 1975, Beckham is five years younger

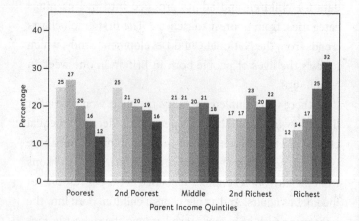

Figure 0.1
Intergenerational mobility in the 1958 birth cohort.[5]

Son earnings quintile:
- Poorest
- 2nd Poorest
- Middle
- 2nd Richest
- Richest

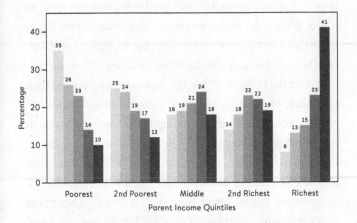

Figure 0.2
Intergenerational mobility in the 1970 birth cohort.[6]

Son earnings quintile:
  Poorest
  2nd Poorest
  Middle
  2nd Richest
  Richest

than the generation tracked in the 1970 cohort study. But it is fair to say that he would be one of the few leaping from the lowest quintile to the highest quintile if a similar graph could be compiled for his 1975 cohort.[7]

David Cameron meanwhile was, in pure income terms at least, a downwardly mobile prime minister. Born in 1966, he is four years older than the cohort summarized above. Earning around £150,000 a year by the time he left office, Cameron would rank comfortably among the top fifth of earners if he featured in these charts. But he was earning far less than his father, who as a successful stockbroker made millions.

The global Beckham brand highlights the huge financial rewards that can be generated in a world economy without national boundaries. But globalization and rapid technological change have created bigger gaps between society's winners and losers. The middle stem of Britain's hourglass economy is disappearing. Britain's rich have been enriched by economic growth. Britain's poor have inherited greater job insecurity and poorer pay.

Our analysis confirms that inequality in Britain has widened as income mobility has fallen. The gap between the high- and low-paid can be measured by the '90:10 earnings ratio'. If the working population is arranged on a ladder with ten rungs, this ratio compares the earnings of those 10 per cent from the top with those 10 per cent from the bottom.[8] It is, broadly speaking, the ratio of what professionals like doctors and lawyers get paid compared with what cleaners and fast-food workers earn. The rungs of the earnings ladder have got wider, as Figure 0.3 shows. In 1980 the

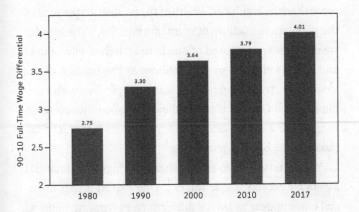

Figure 0.3
90–10 wage differentials, 1980 to 2017.[9]

worker from the top 10 per cent was earning 2.75 times more than the worker 10 per cent from the bottom. By 2017 the difference was 4 times.

It is not just earnings but total wealth – including financial investments and housing – that sets the moneyed elite apart from the rest of us. Wealth inequality is on a different scale of magnitude to 'bog standard' earnings inequality. In 2017 the richest 1,000 people in Britain owned £658 billion – more than the combined wealth of the poorest 40 per cent of the population, made up of 10 million families.[10] The broader wealth class is composed of one in ten families with houses and assets valued at over £1 million. At the bottom of the wealth spectrum, meanwhile, many people live with crippling debt.[11] Our calculations show people on the top-tenth rung of the wealth ladder are over 80 times wealthier than those on the bottom-tenth rung.[12]

We are returning to an age where earnings from financial assets far exceed simple wages.[13] One reason is that financial elites appear to live by different rules – paying minimal tax to maximize their fortunes. It does not help being in the public spotlight. Beckham was refused a knighthood because of the black mark he received for investing in a tax avoidance scheme.[14] Cameron meanwhile was forced to admit that he had benefitted from an offshore trust established by his father to enable wealthy clients to escape paying tax.[15]

Extreme inequalities of wealth and income are inextricably linked with low income mobility. 'You need some inequality to grow [economically],' the economist Thomas Piketty has argued. 'But extreme inequality is not only useless but can be harmful to [economic] growth because it reduces mobility and can lead to political capture of our democratic institutions.'[16]

We are still finding out how extreme inequality, particularly experienced in early life, leads to lower mobility throughout the life course. But one chief mechanism is through an increasingly inequitable education system. Far from acting as the great social leveller, education has been commandeered by the middle classes to retain their advantage from one generation to the next. Our social elites will go to ever greater lengths to ensure their offspring stay ahead.

Once again the Camerons and Beckhams are illustrative of national trends, but with some unexpected twists. David and his wife Samantha attended two of the country's most famous public schools, Eton and Marlborough College.[17] On the face of it the Cameron children have taken a downward generational step in education mobility. Much was made of the then Prime Minister's decision to send his children to a local state primary school. But that would be to misunderstand the range of tactics the privileged deploy to gain the upper hand in the escalating arms race of education. An exclusive faith school in Kensington can be just as good as a private prep school for staying ahead, and away from, the rest.

Beckham bucks British educational traditions. His first steps to success came through on-the-job training rather than academic study.[18] Beckham signed up as a Youth Training Scheme participant or 'YTS' boy – which had become a derisive label by the 1990s. But then Beckham's sponsor was Manchester United Football Club, a world famous sporting institution.[19] It is unusual for someone so successful, even those in sport or the creative arts, to have progressed through a lower-status vocational pathway – still looked down upon by elites groomed via the 'royal academic route'.

Befitting the newly gained status of their parents, Beckham's children meanwhile all attended private schools. The country's leading fee-charging schools boast an incredible record of producing the country's elites, generation after generation. But they encapsulate the powerful forces of economic and education inequality that combine and reinforce each other to limit mobility. Only the richest parents are able to invest in an elite education that ensures their children access the highest wages in a job market rewarding the highly educated.

Class Divides

Social class offers an alternative way of measuring mobility across the generations, categorizing people in ways that go beyond pounds or dollars earned. Occupation-based class measures are used, and advocates of using such measures argue it attempts to relay information about what jobs we do, what education we have had, and the traits, behaviours and attitudes that define who we are – including, for example, the way we speak and dress. A teacher may earn less than other professionals such as doctors and lawyers, but in most people's eyes he or she is quintessentially middle class.

Social class was traditionally broken down into three broad distinctions: working class, middle class and upper class. And when journalists write news stories on social mobility they still turn to an image from a 1966 episode of the BBC's *David Frost* show familiar to most British readers over a certain age.[20] In the 'Class sketch' a tall John Cleese, in a bowler hat, represents the upper classes, Ronnie Barker, the middle classes, and a short Ronnie Corbett, in a cloth cap, the working classes. They each in turn describe their place in society.

Sociologists developed seven new social class groupings to describe the more complex make-up of the population to study mobility across more recent generations.[21] Based on the job or occupation a person holds, these social classes can not only gauge a person's status according to their earnings, but also proxies for their economic security and the degree of autonomy they enjoy in their workplace.

What is striking is that sociologists also observe greater immobility at the top and bottom of the social class hierarchy, despite deploying different measures and methods. One review highlighted 'the social closure at the upper echelons of society and the isolation of those at the bottom', contrasting these extremes with comparatively high levels of mobility elsewhere.[22]

New Order

In 2011 researchers unveiled yet another alternative social-class scheme to better reflect the characteristics that distinguish people in Britain in the early twenty-first century.[23] Analysing the results of the BBC's Great British Class Survey that gathered details on 161,000 people, academics presented a hierarchy of seven new class distinctions. A person's status was assessed not just by their occupation, but by their combined levels of economic capital (their household income and savings), social capital (the networks of people they knew), and cultural capital (their education, behaviours, traits and attitudes).

At the apex of British society is an 'elite' group whose 'sheer economic advantage' sets them apart from the rest of the nation. Made up of chief executives and financial managers alongside traditional professionals such as dentists and barristers, they make up 6 per cent of the population. This exclusive group, educated at elite universities and likely to live in the south-east of England, has restricted upward mobility into its ranks.

At the bottom of the class structure is the 'precariat'. Living precarious lives on a low income and likely to be renting their accommodation and experiencing high levels of insecurity, this group constitutes 15 per cent of the population. It is made up of the unemployed, cleaners, care workers, postal workers and shopkeepers mainly from outside the south-east of England.

Long-range social mobility, rising from the precariat to the elite group, seldom happens. More common is short-range movement between middle-class groupings, enabled by the social and cultural capital accumulated by going to university. These patterns, of particular stickiness at the bottom and top of society, chime with those observed by economists, demonstrated in the U-shaped mobility charts above.

In social-class terms Cameron maintained his family's position at the very apex of society – a pattern that has persisted for several generations. But the Beckhams are the latest examples of new moneyed elites finding the upper rungs of the class ladder a slippery climb. Their supreme wealth and social connections make them a match for anyone in terms of economic and social capital. And they are catching up culturally. Academics have demonstrated that David and Victoria drop the H sounds at the start of words far less often than they used to.[24] The working-class accents that once betrayed their beginnings have been shed. Posh Spice has become Posher Becks.

And yet the denial of Beckham's knighthood suggested the establishment was not quite ready to accept the tattooed national icon into its uppermost ranks. The honours system remains one of the last bastions controlled by the upper social classes. Journalists often ask the age-old question: is Britain still a class-ridden society? It is. It's just that what constitutes class is always changing. Economists' measures of income mobility provide a constant lens to observe an evolving landscape. But class matters.

The Caravan: Relative and Absolute Progress

The tale of the two Davids points to two different social mobility challenges: the millions of adults stuck at the bottom of the social ladder from which Beckham was fortunate to escape; and the retention of social elites at the top of the ladder which Cameron so typifies.

Beckham's journey might be held up as an example of how with enough talent, determination and hard work (and tireless support from dedicated parents), anyone can make it in modern Britain. But it is the exception, not the rule. Much more than we would imagine, we replicate the footsteps of our forebears. Beckham has joined Cameron among the social elites who are incredibly adept at maintaining their advantage from one generation to the next.

These twin challenges highlight another important feature of social mobility: whether we measure it in absolute or relative terms. To understand the difference, a useful metaphor is to imagine the nation as a caravan travelling through the desert. The pace of the travellers as they walk along their journey represents progress in life whether measured by income, social class or education. An increase in absolute mobility would see everyone – the poor at the rear, and the rich pulling away at the front – quicken their pace and reach a better destination than their forebears. But no one would change their relative position.

An increase in relative mobility would see formerly under-nourished but naturally strong travellers at the back overtake people in front of them. Improving relative mobility without an improvement in absolute mobility is a zero-sum game – one person's gain is another's loss in life's rankings.

Ideally we would want a society that had high levels of mobility in both absolute and relative terms: all people are moving more quickly, but people are leapfrogging others as well. We want the strongest walkers, irrespective of where they started, at the front to lead us on the best possible path forward.

In modern Britain, widening income and wealth inequality makes changing places more difficult. The rich have been pulling further away from the poorer people behind them: as this happens, it is harder for people to catch up. At the same time, a lack of supplies (due to falling median real wages) means that the pace of the caravan for most people has been slowing, and everyone is doing all they can to retain their place.

An obvious improvement for all travellers would be to narrow the lengthening gaps in life's caravan. But it is difficult to reach consensus on this: those at the front want the freedom to stretch out; they believe others can join them if they make enough effort. Narrowing gaps, they argue, would remove any incentives to strive harder, leading to lazy walkers slowing everyone down.

Improving relative mobility, ensuring the fittest people from all positions in society have the option of getting to the front of the caravan, would produce not only the fittest leaders, but also those who understand the plight of fellow travellers in the distance behind them. What is clear is that walkers require a good education, the nourishment needed to progress, but also a helping hand to traverse a rough terrain.

The lack of movement in who gets where in the world – particularly when people are stuck at the bottom and the top – costs the nation dear in wasted talent. Shrinking opportunities overall, the growing forces of globalization, automation and widening inequality, makes the goal of improving social mobility in Britain tough. Our caravan is walking into a perfect storm.

Failure to do something about this will store up greater social and economic problems for future generations. It will ultimately unravel the cohesive society we all want to live in. Without drawing on talents from all backgrounds our elites become detached from, and disinterested in, the rest of society.

David Beckham's rise highlights why mobility is so often a one-way street. Britain's social mobility problem defies normal logic. What goes up doesn't always come down. David and his wife Victoria have devoted considerable resources to ensure that their four children secure opportunities that are increasingly out of reach for the rest of the population. All three of the Beckhams' sons, for example, were enrolled into the exclusive Arsenal Football Club academy – an impossible dream for most boys and girls. Fashion, music and modelling careers have been mooted. In Britain's bleak mobility climate, children outside these elite cliques have little hope of accessing these opportunities, irrespective of how much talent or work ethic they may have.

Cameron's aides advised him against too much talk about social mobility for fear of attracting attention to his privileged upbringing. But Cameron said the Conservatives were now 'the party of aspiration'. 'Britain has the lowest social mobility in the developed world,' he told the Conservative Party conference in 2015. 'Here, the salary you earn is more linked to what your father got paid than in any other major country.'[25] Yet for all the rhetoric, in office Cameron dismissed concerns about socially selective schools, unpaid internships and low inheritance tax. He will be remembered as the leader of a detached metropolitan elite who misjudged the mood of the people when they voted to leave Europe.

Cameron's advisers came up with a clever phrase for the Prime Minister. It demonstrated his aspirations for a classless society where background does not matter: 'It's where you're going to, not where you're from that counts.' But the mantra was a fallacy. In Britain it has become increasingly the case that where you come from – who you are born to and where you are born – matters more than ever for where you are going to.

PART ONE

Social Mobility and Inequality

Mobility and Inequality

At international conferences academics from different countries can be heard asking one important question: 'How big is your beta?' The measure economists use to gauge the mobility of different nations is called the intergenerational elasticity (or IGE). In many studies it is given the symbol beta, β. The number reveals how sticky different nations are: how likely children are as adults to be in the same earnings or income bracket as their parents.[1]

For those unacquainted with the technical details of betas or IGEs, the question is put more simply: how low is social mobility in a country such as Britain? It is usually accompanied by a much harder question: how much more mobile could the country be? It is why a twenty-page report by London School of Economics researchers published in 2005 by the Sutton Trust made such an impact. It found that Britain (along with the United States), came bottom of the international league table of income mobility.[2] Who you were born to mattered more in Britain (and the US) in predicting what you were likely to earn as an adult than in Canada, Germany, Sweden, Norway, Denmark and Finland.

Britons and Americans from poorer families found it harder than those in other nations to climb the income ladder and earn more money than their parents. 'America and Britain have the highest intergenerational persistence,' concluded the paper. Compared to most countries, the British beta was big.

The LSE economists concluded not only that income mobility was low in Britain by international standards, but that it had declined across recent generations. Income mobility was lower for the British generation born in 1970 compared with that born in 1958. Children who grew up in poorer homes in the 1970s were more likely than the previous generation to end up relatively poor as adults. For all the talk of breaking down ingrained social-class barriers, Britain, at least according to the barometer of earnings, had become less mobile for people entering the labour market in the 1990s compared with those getting jobs in the 1980s.

The downward trend is shown by comparing the long-range mobility measure for children growing up in respective generations born in 1958 and 1970. Few people would be expected to make a dramatic transition during their lifetime. Yet 17 per cent of those born in 1958 in the bottom quarter of family incomes did so, ending up among the top quarter of earners by their late thirties. These odds, of living the equivalent of the American dream, had measurably declined for those born just twelve years later in 1970. Only 11 per cent born in the poorest households then had moved up into the highest earners as adults by their late thirties (by which time most people had reached their maximum earnings).

Prime ministers come and go, but all seem to return to the damning LSE findings as they outline their hopes for a more mobile society. 'This slender analysis has, arguably, had more influence on public debate than any academic paper of the past twenty years,' the journalist David Goodhart has claimed.[3] Government reviews have been announced, papers published, commissions created.[4] Improving social mobility became the principal goal of the Government's social policy.[5] Yet we appear to be no closer to unlocking Britain's rigid society.[6]

International Comparisons

Many subsequent studies have confirmed Britain's low intergenerational mobility.[7] An international review by the OECD concluded that Britain was at the bottom of the income mobility league table, 'with around 50 per cent of a person's income explained by his or her parents' income'. In Denmark, Norway, Finland and Canada, parental income explained less than 20 per cent of a child's eventual earnings.[8] On this measure, British people experienced only half the mobility enjoyed by their Scandinavian or Canadian counterparts.

An intergenerational income elasticity of 1 would mean there was no mobility at all: all poor children would become poor adults and all rich children would become rich adults. Everyone would stay in the same position in the nation's income distribution as their parents. An elasticity of zero would mean complete mobility with no relationship between family background and the adult outcomes of children. A child born into poverty would have exactly the same chance of becoming rich in later life as a child born to rich parents.

Britain, according to the latest estimates shown in

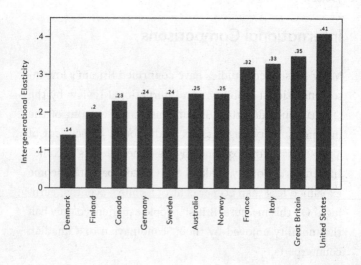

Figure 1.1
Intergenerational differences in intergenerational elasticity.[9]

Figure 1.1, has by international standards a high intergenerational elasticity of 0.35.[10] By contrast, the earnings elasticity in Denmark is 0.14 – around a third of that in Britain.

Researchers have also been able to consider intergenerational correlations in terms of ranks.[11] By ordering parents' and children's income levels from the lowest to the highest, it is possible to obtain rank measures for both generations, and researchers have argued that rank–rank correlations offer robust measures of the extent of intergenerational mobility. The correlations corroborate the elasticity patterns. Britain remains low in the advanced economies' league table of social mobility.

Anglophone Comparisons

Educationalists have to tread carefully when interpreting international comparisons. Countless excursions have been organized to stand-out education performers such as Finland or Singapore, only to discover that the societies are different in many dimensions to Britain; it is hard to find any meaningful lessons that apply back home. Context matters.

But what is striking about the international comparisons of income mobility is that similar countries have different betas: Australia and Canada have lower betas and more income mobility than Britain and the United States. This is despite a shared history, common language and cultures. The differences suggest Britain is less mobile than it could be. For policy makers they prompt tantalizing questions: could Britain learn any lessons from Canada or Australia, and improve its mobility levels?

One suggestion is that smaller gaps in educational achievement between the rich and poor in Australia and Canada lies behind their higher mobility levels.[12] Children from poorer families in Australia and Canada have a greater chance of doing well at school, getting into university and earning more in later in life than children in Britain and the US. And this is the case even though Britain and the US spend a greater proportion of their GDP on schooling.

For the most part, Australians and Canadians do not suffer the same education extremes observed in Britain. Fewer young people are missing out on the most basic skills needed to get on in life; and at the top of the social-class pyramid there is nothing remotely resembling Britain's powerful private-school elite.

The environments in which children grow up are also different. Canada and Australia have smaller gaps between the rich and poor than those in Britain and the US. Australian and Canadian graduates do not command the comparatively high salaries enjoyed by their British or American counterparts.

Children in Britain and the US meanwhile are at least twice as likely to be born to teenage mothers as children in Australia and Canada.[13] Being born to a single teenage mother is one of the strongest predictors of performing poorly in school in any country – and of earning less in the labour market as an adult. Canada and Australia are far less densely populated than Britain and are not dominated by one major international metropolis (London). Some believe it is more simple: Canadians and Australians do not suffer the same class and cultural divide that has forever obsessed and defined Brits.

How Much Higher (or Lower)?

What higher levels of social or income mobility could Britain realistically aim towards? There is no straightforward answer to this question: no one knows what the optimal level for any country is, and from the current state of research we do not have a good economic means of thinking about what that optimal level might be. But we do know otherwise similar countries such as Australia and Canada have significantly higher mobility.

Few people would advocate a world of total social mobility where a person's chances of success in later life were uncorrelated with the parental home they grew up in. And extremely unpalatable policies would be required to create such a society: separating children from their parents at birth and randomly allocating work opportunities, for example. But the international comparisons of income mobility indicate what improvement might just be possible in Britain. On the flipside they show just how much worse it could get.

Stanford University economist Raj Chetty and his fellow US researchers used the long-range or 'rags to riches' measure of income mobility to ask how realistic the American dream is for a number of different countries. They calculated the proportion of children born to parents in the bottom poorest fifth of households who leap into the top richest fifth of homes as adults. The results are presented in Figure 1.2.[14]

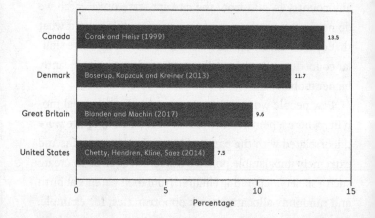

Figure 1.2
Probability of moving from bottom to top quintile.[15]

A society of complete mobility, in which background and outcomes were unrelated, would see 20 per cent of the population making this bottom to top journey. A world of absolute rigidity would be signalled by a rags-to-riches metric of zero, where none of those from the poorest backgrounds made it into the richest homes in adult life.

In Britain 9.6 per cent of people who began life in the bottom fifth of the income distribution made it into the top fifth of incomes by their late 30s. In Canada, a higher percentage – 13.5 per cent – achieve the American dream. Given the cultural, historical and economic similarities of the two countries this higher level of upward mobility would seem to be a realistic, if ambitious, aim for Britain. It would require, at least according to this measure, a significant improvement – around 40 per cent up – on current mobility levels in our country.

The Canadian figure is similar to the highest levels of long-range income mobility observed for 'high opportunity' cities in the United States, including San Francisco for example at 12.2 per cent.[16] We will return to these local variations in income mobility in Chapter 3 as they offer further clues to what drivers may lead to more healthy levels of social mobility.

On the other hand in the United States overall (where the American dream was born of course), only 7.5 per cent of people make it from the bottom to the top of society. Given the common characteristics of the US and Britain, the danger for Britain is it slips down further to this lower level of income mobility – equivalent to a 20 per cent drop on current levels.

America's 'low opportunity' areas have long-range mobility as low as 5.5 per cent. That is equivalent to a 40 per cent drop on current levels in Britain. Unless we change matters, the fear is Britain could drop down to these levels of rigidity and stay rooted to the bottom of the international league table. Even more British lives would be wasted – our economy would weaken and society would become more divided. Success in life would be determined even more by who you are born to, rather than individual talent or hard work.

The *Great Gatsby* Curve

The Great Gatsby by F. Scott Fitzgerald is one of the great works of American literature, capturing a lost age of excess during the United States of the 1920s, prior to the Wall Street crash. In modern-day America the magnitude of the income gaps between rich and poor has returned to the levels experienced nearly a century ago. For the Roaring Twenties read the great divides of the early twenty-first century.

These parallels were thrust into the social mobility debate when Alan Krueger, a Princeton academic serving as President Barack Obama's chief economic adviser, unveiled the 'the *Great Gatsby* Curve'. It was unusual for a White House official to give a speech ahead of the President's State of the Union Address. What Krueger had to say was controversial. Here was a senior US Government adviser conceding publicly the American dream is little more than a myth for many citizens.[17] The implication of the *Great Gatsby* Curve is that today's stark inequality harms future social mobility.

Krueger's graph (redrawn in Figure 1.3 with more recent data) was based on data originally gathered by the Canadian economist Miles Corak, comparing income inequality and income mobility levels for a number of rich countries. On the horizontal axis is the official Gini coefficient, which measures the level of income inequality: the higher the coefficient, the bigger the income gap between the richest and poorest in society. Krueger used inequality measures registered when children were growing up in order to capture their impact on their lives. On the vertical axis is the 'intergenerational earnings elasticity' – the IGE or beta for each country. As we have seen, this measure signals how sticky or immobile a society is, comparing one generation with the previous one. The higher this number, the lower the earnings mobility across generations.

As you can see, the Curve (actually a straight line) shows more unequal societies are less mobile. Put simply, when the rungs of the income ladder are wide, the chances of climbing the ladder are lower. Ominously, the Curve suggests less mobility for future generations in Britain and the United States, nations that are particularly unequal and immobile by international standards.

The Curve demonstrates just how powerful a memorable title can be. F. Scott Fitzgerald's working title was 'Among the Ash Heaps and Millionaires'. Krueger says, 'I venture the hypothesis that had he stuck with that title no one would recall Jay Gatsby today, and the *Great Gatsby* curve would have been christened with a different name.'[18] Krueger's research assistants came up with the name after being offered a bottle of New Jersey wine to find a catchy title.

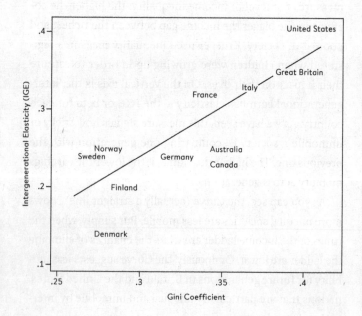

Figure 1.3
The *Great Gatsby* curve.[19]

Another link was the fact that F. Scott Fitzgerald had studied at Princeton.

Corak's statistics, carefully estimated over many years, chimed with other studies. In 2009 Australian academics produced a graph entitled 'more inequality, less social mobility'.[20] A similar graph is presented in the book *The Spirit Level*.[21] The LSE report on Britain's low social mobility meanwhile cited two main drivers – widening income and education inequalities.

But the Curve charts a correlation between two statistics, not a causal relationship. This is an important point. If it was that simple, improving mobility would be a straightforward task of raising taxes to redistribute money. Income gaps would be reduced and life prospects instantly boosted for people from all backgrounds. But this would ignore a critical point: it is how money is spent that decides who progresses up, or slides down, the income ladder. Richer families deploy their resources – most noticeably on the education of their offspring – in ways that lead to enhanced life prospects compared with families from poorer backgrounds.

But Krueger is convinced inequality does lead to lower mobility: 'I do think it is a causal relationship. I think the research points fairly strongly at that. Another way of thinking about this is that if it is a causal relationship then this relationship is exactly what one would expect.'[22] The *Great Gatsby* Curve suggests the political debates over whether to aim for equality of outcome or equality of opportunity are a false dichotomy. The two principles are inextricably related: extreme inequality of incomes at one point in time leads to greater inequality of opportunity over time which in turn leads to widening gaps between the rich and poor. This seems plausible, given that privileged elites over successive generations may be less inclined to support the redistributive policies that would give those lower down society's ranks a greater chance of displacing them at the top.

Moving Up (or Down) the *Great Gatsby* Curve

The *Great Gatsby* Curve suggests that wide gaps between the rich and poor, if left unchecked, lead to more rigid societies. And the problem for Britain is we sit (alongside the US) in the worst place: the upper right-hand quadrant of the *Great Gatsby* graph of high inequality and low mobility. If the relationship continues to hold true for current generations of children and young people then it does not bode well for future prospects for social mobility. As we have seen, there could be as much as a 40 per cent drop on current mobility levels, given the data from other countries.

How is it that wide gaps between the rich and poor lead to lower social mobility levels? Partly this is because in Britain it is simply harder to climb the income ladder than say in Canada or Denmark, as growing income inequality has made the steps much wider. But it's also likely to be due to the unequal forces that shape the lives of children from different backgrounds.

Richer children are more likely to benefit from a stable, supportive and less stressful family environment during their early years. As they grow their parents are adept at deploying considerable time and resources to enable their children to access the best schools, private tutors and universities in Britain. The education system has become the vehicle through which inequality of incomes drives inequality of opportunities. And this appears to be a particularly British phenomenon: larger gaps in educational achievement are observed between poorer pupils and their more privileged peers in this country compared with those in Australia and Canada.[23]

Widening Wealth Gaps

Inequality is multi-dimensional. It's not just about the pay we receive but the assets we own – cultural, social and financial. Growing inequality of wealth has consolidated the position of the elites. Not only do they benefit from the high returns from their financial investments, but the expensive homes they own enable their sons and daughters to access the country's best jobs in the heart of London. Bricks and mortar have created new obstacles to social mobility.

Another signal of Britain's increasing rigidity is that the likelihood of getting on the housing ladder for the first time has decreased for recent generations. There has been a drop in 'home ownership' mobility – mirroring the decline in income mobility.[24] For many people in developed economies, housing wealth is the largest component of their overall wealth. Changes in the extent of home ownership mobility also reflect changes in wealth mobility.

We chart this generational shift in Figure 1.4, comparing the two generations, those born in 1958 and in 1970, at age 42. It traces people in both generations according to one

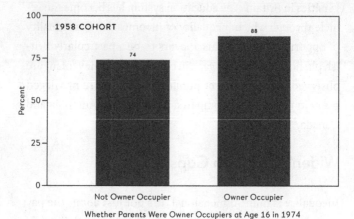

Figure 1.4
Percentage of owner-occupiers at age 42 in two generations.[25]

single factor: 'owner occupancy' – whether they or their parents owned their own home.

A bigger divide has emerged in the chances of becoming a home owner for the more recent generation. For those born in 1958, there was a gap of 14 percentage points in the likelihood of becoming an owner-occupier between those brought up in rented accommodation and those from home-owning families. But for those born in 1970 the gap had stretched to 22 percentage points. 'Generation rent' is just another manifestation of low social mobility in Britain.

Krueger uses *The Great Gatsby* to draw parallels on rising income inequality in modern society with the great divides from a century before; Thomas Piketty instead shows how the accumulation of wealth is once again limiting intergenerational mobility in the twenty-first century, as it did in the early nineteenth century. In his book *Capital in the Twenty-First Century*, the French economist references the novels of Jane Austen and Honoré de Balzac.[26] Austen's novels reveal the rigid class structure of English society, dominated by powerful dynasties owning vast assets. In Balzac's 1835 novel *Le Père Goriot*, a young law student, Rastignac, faces a dilemma: either he marries a rich heiress to gain wealth, or pursues a much harder life on his own to realize his dream of becoming a professional lawyer. Early twenty-first-century Britain is beginning to resemble nineteenth-century France, with inherited wealth making up an increasing share of national income. *C'est la vie*.

Finally, increasing gaps between the rich and poor appear to depress not only relative income mobility but absolute mobility levels as well. Once again the warning signs come from the other side of the Atlantic. Half of Americans are now worse off than their parents.[27] The American dream of just doing better, let alone climbing the social ladder, is dying.

Three-quarters of this decline is down to widening gaps in income inequality; a quarter is down to lower economic growth.[28] The implications for government policy are profound. Simply boosting the national economy, even if it could be achieved, would have little impact on absolute social mobility levels; it has to be inclusive growth, involving and benefitting all. In the next chapter we will show how younger Britons are also facing the prospect of earning less than their parents. This in turn means fewer are likely to climb an already steep income ladder. For the ill-fated generations of the future it will be an era of shrinking opportunity.

CHAPTER 2

Rising and Falling Economic Tides

The story of Britain's low income mobility is anchored to the ups and downs of Britain's economy since the Second World War. In the mid-twentieth century, lifted by a wave of post-war optimism, economists became convinced of the 'rising tide lifts all boats' hypothesis: the booming economy would bring increasing prosperity and higher living standards to all sections of society.[1]

And for a time Britain during the 1950s and 1960s was in many respects living the dream, summed up by one famous speech by Prime Minister Harold Macmillan in 1957. 'Let us be frank about it: most of our people have never had it so good,' he told the nation. 'Go round the country, go to the industrial towns, go to the farms and you will see a state of prosperity such as we have never had in my lifetime – nor indeed in the history of this country.'[2]

Social mobility prospects in absolute terms were indeed buoyant. Between 1950 and 1973 the country experienced economic growth of 3 per cent per year; between 1950 and 1969 the unemployment rate averaged just 1.6 per cent.[3] Everybody's incomes grew as prosperity was shared, and inequality stayed constant.[4] The younger generation entered a labour market abundant with good jobs and decent pay.

Yet at the same time there was little evidence of upward mobility from the lower rungs of the social ladder. 'We are strictly second class. We don't understand why we should be on dead-end street,' sang Ray Davies, lead singer of the Kinks, in a song about the hopelessness of the British lower classes.[5] It was a typically astute observation: swinging London was mostly a middle-class affair.

The global crash of the early 1970s poured cold water on any idealistic notions of a world of inexorably improving levels of absolute social mobility. Britain was plunged into economic gloom amid a global recession. The world economy slowed down, and stagflation – the unheard-of phenomenon of simultaneously rising inflation and unemployment – kicked in. The cost of living got higher and getting jobs got harder. This unexpected combination, exacerbated by the big oil price rises of 1973–4, caused Britain and other countries to sink to economic lows not seen for decades.

In hindsight the golden post-war era had been little more than a honeymoon period before harsh realities returned. The 1970s decade is remembered for strikes, football hooligans, power cuts, the three-day week and the 'winter of discontent'. Inflation rose to double figures, at its peak reaching over 25 per cent; the unemployment rate rose to levels not witnessed since the 1930s. Alternative musicians of the day, just as in the 1960s, voiced the younger generation's disenchantment with Britain's rigid society, now against a backdrop of the deteriorating economic conditions enveloping the country. 'And there is no future in England's dreaming' declared the Sex Pistols in 1977. 'God Save the Queen' was a song attacking the establishment's mistreatment of the working classes.[6]

Fanciful notions of rising tides raising all boats had all but crashed on the rocks. At the same time, the 1970s did not see any discernible changes in inequality of incomes, nor in relative social mobility levels. The rungs of society's ladder were no wider, but movement between them was no greater.

Growing Divides

By the 1980s an alternative theory gained acceptance: 'trickle-down economics'. This, economists and politicians argued, would mean increasing resources attracted by small, wealthy elites would 'trickle down' to benefit everyone. Growing gaps between the rich and poor were acceptable, and even encouraged through lower taxes for high earners, as they would spur more investment and hiring, igniting the economy into action.

The 1980s, 1990s and 2000s were Britain's decades of rising inequality. The deep recession of the early 1980s hit the economy hard and parts of the country, especially those that had previously benefitted from the manufacturing industry, never recovered. Inequality increased rapidly during the decade, and throughout the earnings distribution. The result was the 'fanning out' of the earnings distribution, shown in Figure 2.1 for selected percentiles of weekly wages through the 1980s.

The 1990s and 2000s saw the wealthiest in society pulling further and further away from everyone else. Increases in

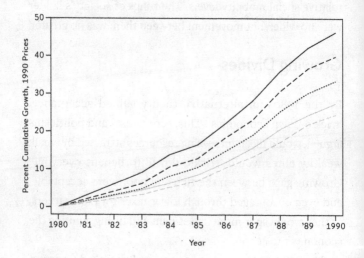

Figure 2.1
Real wages in the 1980s.[7]

——— 90th Percentile
– – – 75th Percentile
·········· 50th Percentile
——— 25th Percentile
– – – 10th Percentile

inequality during this period occurred in the 'upper tail' of highest earners, with less change for the bottom half of the earnings distribution.[8] Figure 2.2 shows that real wages grew similarly for those at the 10th, 25th and 50th percentiles of the distribution but increased much more rapidly for those at the 75th and the 90th percentiles.

And there were different trends for individual workers' earnings, compared with family incomes. Both were at higher levels by 2010 than thirty years previously. But while earnings inequality rose throughout the thirty-year period, most of the rise in family income inequality happened in the 1980s. These patterns in part reflected changes in family composition. For example, there were more dual-earner families by the 2000s.[9] Nonetheless, inequality in earnings and household income were both a lot higher by 2016. We can compare those on the top-tenth rung of the income ladder and those on the bottom-tenth rung – the 90:10 ratio – for full-time weekly earnings and net household incomes. They were 2.8 and 3.1 respectively in 1980; by 2016 they were 3.4 and 3.9.

As the divide between rich and poor rose, the chances of climbing the income ladder fell. Trickle-down economics had in reality led to ever greater economic divides, as those already rich accrued a greater share of the economic spoils and the poor increasingly lost out. The wealthy were watertight. The next generation inherited the worse of all worlds: high levels of inequality, low levels of social mobility and bleak prospects for economic growth.

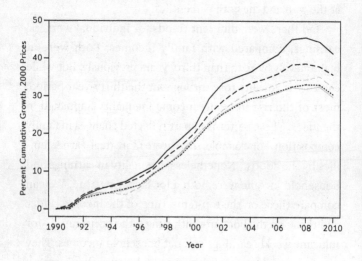

Figure 2.2
Real wages in the 1990s and 2000s.[10]

——— 90th Percentile
– – – 75th Percentile
·········· 50th Percentile
— — 25th Percentile
—·—· 10th Percentile

Falling Absolute Mobility

In the wake of the global financial crisis of 2007–8, Britain's economic growth would be best described as sluggish. National productivity stalled and real wages fell. Fewer people were unemployed, but people were taking home lower incomes than they did before, and often working in insecure jobs with scant hope of career progression.

The problem is what economists have referred to as Britain's productivity puzzle: while there were more jobs in the economy, the country's overall economic productivity stagnated.[11] Figure 2.3 shows that UK productivity in 2017 was 20 per cent below the long-term trend in growth it was on prior to the 2007–8 downturn.

Workers' wages had declined in real terms. And to an unprecedented extent since comparable wage data has existed.[12] Figure 2.4 shows the scale of the falls experienced by workers since 2008: the median worker's wages decreased by 5 per cent in real terms.[13] Men did significantly worse than women, but both experienced real wage falls at the median over the ten years after 2008. They were worse off than their counterparts in the labour market ten years earlier.

Declining real wages signal falling absolute social mobility. The pay packets of today's generation are worth less as they fail to keep up with the rising cost of living; in contrast their parents, three decades earlier, were enjoying increasing wages compared with the generation before.

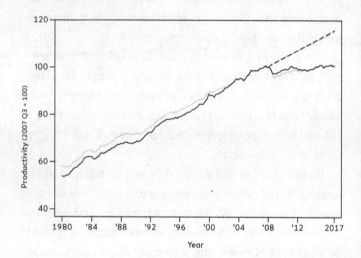

Figure 2.3
UK productivity, 1980–2017.[12]

——— Output per hour, Y/H
——— Output per worker, Y/L
– – – Y/H 1994/2007 trend
– – – Y/L 1994/2007 trend

All Median	-6%
Male Median	-10%
Female Median	-2%

Figure 2.4
Real wage changes, 2008–17.[15]

Many children's living standards are no better than their parents were.[16]

This economic era is that of a falling tide in which the smallest, most vulnerable boats are sinking fastest. In decades past people on the wrong side of widening income gaps could console themselves that their wages had at least risen in real terms. Now, to add insult to injury, wages have fallen, meaning most people are now materially worse off than they were fifteen years ago. Economic boom has been replaced by economic gloom.

These economic trends chime with the narrative from a rich academic literature on social-class mobility produced by sociologists over several decades. The evidence points to a post-war boom in absolute mobility levels.[17] This was a golden age during which a high proportion of people enjoyed upward mobility, filling the new professional and managerial jobs created by an expanding British economy. Towards the end of the twentieth century rates of upward mobility among men stabilized. For women, modest increases in social mobility continued. Meanwhile, relative rates of intergenerational class mobility remained constant.[18]

The unsettling experience of downward mobility is becoming increasingly common for more recent generations of both men and women. A study led by Oxford University tracking four successive post-war generations found around three-quarters of men and women alike ended up by their late twenties or thirties in a different social class to the one they were born into. This was as true for those born in 1946 as it was for those born between 1980 and 1984. But as the British economy had slowed down, the direction of mobility had flipped. Falling down, rather than climbing up, the social ladder had become a more common experience.

The report laid bare the extreme class inequalities in the prospects of ending up on the social ladder's highest rungs. The chances of a child with a higher professional father ending up in a similar position rather than in a working-class position were up to twenty times greater than these same chances for a child with a working-class father. The class divide endures.

'Politicians are saying that a new generation of young people don't have the same opportunities for social advancement as their parents, and these results seem to bear that out,' concluded the researchers. 'The emerging situation is one for which there is little historical precedent and that carries potentially far-reaching political and wider social implications.'[19]

Lost Ladders of Opportunity

As the sociologists suggest, the young generation growing up in early 21st-century Britain have been hit hardest. Their real wages have fallen by more than other groups. The median real wage for those aged under twenty-five in 2017 is equivalent to that recorded in 1997. Young people's earning levels have been frozen for two decades.

The wage freeze for the young meanwhile has restricted their ability to get on the housing ladder compared with previous generations. In 1994–5 42 per cent of those under twenty-five were private renters; by 2013–14 this had climbed to 67 per cent.[20] They really are on dead-end street. They are spending more of their diminishing income for a roof over their heads. The golden age of the 1950s and 1960s has turned into the bleak age of the early twenty-first century.

Britain's booming gig economy has created an employment underclass (or precariat) lacking security, progression or rights: young, poorly educated, and on short-term and temporary contracts (or gigs). Work practices at the Ubers, Sports Directs and Deliveroos of the world are reminiscent of the work conditions in Victorian times.[21] The increased use of 'zero-hours contracts' – for which employers are not obliged to provide any minimum working hours – harks back to the days of queuing for jobs on the docks a hundred years ago. In 2017, an estimated 1.3 million people were 'employed' in the gig economy.[22]

Declining union membership is another signal of the reduced bargaining power of workers. In 2015 only 13 per cent of workers aged 16–30 were trade union members, compared with 36 per cent for workers aged 50 and over. In 1990, 30 per cent of workers aged less than 30 were trade union members.

In stark contrast to workplace training in countries like Germany and Switzerland, Britain's apprenticeship system is broken: too many apprenticeships are sub-standard, offering no progression, and are undervalued by employers.[23] A credible alternative vocational stream to challenge the high-status academic path has yet to materialize.

Many low-skilled jobs have been lost in Britain to lower-paid workers overseas. Globalization impacted many routine jobs, but automation threatens paraprofessional jobs as well: accountants, insurance underwriters, bank tellers, financial analysts, as well as construction workers and farmers. Some warn the rapid rise of robots and artificial intelligence will create 'an elite high-skilled group dominating the higher echelon of society and a lower-skilled, low-income group with limited prospects of upward mobility and facing a broken social ladder'.[24]

Those from poorer backgrounds are more likely to be cast adrift in this fast-changing workplace. They have fewer opportunities to reskill or retrain. They are less likely to acquire life skills valued by employers such as confidence, creativity and communication. They have fewer contacts and connections. A confluence of currents is washing away their prospects. The younger generation has never had it so bad.

The Price of Immobility

It is difficult not to avoid a sinking feeling about Britain's social mobility prospects. The country is missing out on our biggest talent pool, instead fishing in the same small pond generation after generation. The argument for greater social mobility for Britain has become an economic as well as social one – mirroring the debate in the United States. Studies estimate that modest increases in Britain's social mobility would lead to an annual increase in the country's GDP of between 2 and 4 per cent.[25] To put these figures into context, a 4 per cent loss in GDP would be suffered in a major recession. In more mobile societies jobs are filled by those with the highest level of potential to perform well in that role, rather than someone who may be less well suited but better connected. Enhanced social mobility could solve Britain's productivity puzzle.

A second way of assessing the economic benefits from improving social mobility exploits the link between mobility and income inequality we charted in the *Great Gatsby* Curve. If social mobility levels in Britain were improved to those in Canada, for example, its Gini coefficient would be four percentage points lower.[26] This would raise GDP per head by 4.4 per cent since we also know one percentage point reduction in the Gini coefficient increases GDP per capita in the short run by 1.1 per cent.[27] The benefits from reduced inequality show bigger effects in the long run. Improving social mobility makes for good economic policy. As Nobel Laureate Joseph Stiglitz says, 'another world is possible': one where living standards and well-being are higher as a result of greater mobility and lower inequality.[28] We will find in the next chapter that this applies not only nationally but at a local and regional level as well.

Mapping Mobility

Big Data Hunter

The world's leading researchers are constantly on the look-out for new data. The better and more extensive the statistics, the more accurate and powerful their academic work will be. This is true in many academic fields, but particularly so in the study of social mobility, where researchers have to rely on national data sets spanning entire populations.

This is why the achievements of Raj Chetty are so impressive. Chetty, who was born in New Delhi and moved to the US when he was nine, became one of the youngest ever professors at Harvard. Now at Stanford, he has demonstrated great skill in hunting down and interrogating 'big data' – huge datasets containing millions of statistics.[1] And that statistical power enabled Chetty and his fellow researchers to produce a landmark study that catapulted social mobility research into a new dimension.

Other researchers are still scratching their heads trying to fathom how Chetty and his fellow economist Emmanuel Saez persuaded the US Treasury Department's Office of Tax Policy to hand over the tax records of 40 million Americans.[2] Government tax data is notoriously hard to access. And these records were gold dust as they linked adults' tax returns with their social security numbers – revealing information about their circumstances as children.

Chetty's treasure chest of data revealed for the first time a detailed map of upward mobility levels for different cities, counties and states across America (defined by 741 different 'commuting zones').[3] Using the records of the incomes of 40 million children growing up in the 1980s and their parents they produced a modern day Domesday Book documenting the best and worst places for social mobility in the US. The findings enable us to get closer to finding out what we might do to improve social mobility.

'It's encouraging as it suggests that the problem is tractable and we can do something in local communities to have a meaningful impact on opportunity,' says Chetty. 'What we see in the data is that it is much more of a local problem: the San Francisco dream versus the Atlanta dream; the situation is different across small places.'[4]

The economists looked in particular at the chances of children experiencing the so-called 'long range' mobility we considered in Chapter 1 – moving up from the lowest income bracket in childhood to the highest income bracket in adulthood.[5] This is moving from the sticky bottom end of society to the sticky top.

They found poor children who grow up in certain American cities and states have much better odds of escaping poverty than similar poor children elsewhere. In the highest-mobility areas of the United States, more than one in ten children with parents in the bottom quintile of the income distribution reached the top quintile by adulthood. In the lowest-mobility areas, less than one in twenty poor children reached the top quintile.

As Figure 3.1 shows, in cities such as San Jose (where children have a 12.9 per cent chance of becoming a high earner as an adult), San Francisco (a 12.2 per cent chance), Seattle (a 10.9 per cent chance), and parts of New York (a 10.5 per cent chance), the likelihood of climbing the income ladder are on a par with socially mobile countries such as Denmark or Canada.

But for others such as Atlanta (where children have a 4.5 per cent chance of becoming a high earner as an adult), Cleveland (a 5.1 per cent chance) and Chicago (a 6.5 per cent chance), levels of mobility are depressingly low. Poor children living in areas in the west and north-east of the country were found to have the best chances of making it to the top; those in the south-east of the country and the 'Rust Belt' had the worst chances.

Baltimore, Maryland is a place of scant opportunity – in real life as well as fiction. The American HBO television drama *The Wire* depicted Baltimore's brutal gangland battles, shining a light on how people are affected by the places they grow up in – and the inadequacy of the public policies they experience.[6] For British audiences it was a delicious irony that one of the main characters, Jimmy McNulty, a detective in the Baltimore Police Department, is played by an Old Etonian English actor, Dominic West. But that is another story we shall return to.

According to the American political scientist Francis Fukuyama, the show was a powerful indictment of failed

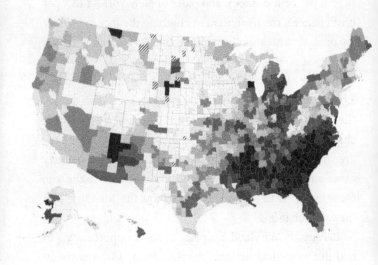

Figure 3.1
The geography of upward mobility in America.[7]

> 16.8%
12.9% – 16.8%
11.3% – 12.9%
9.9% – 11.3%
9.0% – 9.9%
8.1% – 9.0%
7.1% – 8.1%
6.1% – 7.1%
4.8% – 6.1%
< 4.8%
Missing Data

social policies – on education, housing, employment and crime prevention: 'The drug trade, single-parent families, unsafe neighbourhoods and poor, under-resourced schools are the results less of poor individual choices than of dysfunctional institutions. If we are going to change any of the outcomes on the ground, we cannot rely simply on self-help.'[8]

Moving to Opportunity

The ultimate dream for researchers is to find the real reasons behind social trends – discounting all other possible explanations. The question for the Chetty team was whether the place you grow up in has a genuine causal impact on your life chances. They were able to provide an answer by analysing data from the Moving to Opportunity (MTO) experiment in the US in the 1990s.

The initial results of the MTO research were disappointing. Families in high-poverty housing projects were offered housing vouchers to move to lower-poverty neighbourhoods. In New York, for example, many MTO participants moved from Martin Luther King Towers, a housing development in Harlem, ten miles north to Wakefield in the North Bronx. Ten miles can make a big difference in New York. Yet when the researchers compared what happened to families who moved with those who stayed they found little difference: the reading and maths scores of children and the future earnings of adults were the same.[9]

But when Chetty looked into what happened to children who moved when they were under the age of thirteen, a different picture emerged.[10] Younger children who moved to better-off neighbourhoods were more likely to go to college; they were also more likely to earn more in their twenties compared with children left behind.

Not only this, the uplift in fortunes was felt for future generations – what Chetty calls 'downstream impacts on family structure'. Girls who moved into better neighbourhoods were more likely to stay in the same relationship as adults when they had children: the grandchildren of movers in the experiment were more likely to be raised by two parents.

'It really seems like childhood environment is what is driving these differences across areas, moving to a better area as an adult doesn't seem to do a lot for you in terms of economic outcome,' says Chetty. 'The data shows we can do something about upward mobility. Every extra year of childhood spent in a better neighbourhood seems to matter.'[11]

The middle-class communities in lower poverty areas did not suffer as a result of their new neighbours. 'There is no smoking gun evidence in the data that the rich tend to do worse in more integrated cities,' says Chetty. Place matters: where you are born as well as who you are born to has a profound impact on your life prospects.

England's Mobility Map

England's education equivalent of the Chetty chart is a map published by the Sutton Trust education foundation revealing the places with the biggest academic divides.[12] The Social Mobility Index ranked parliamentary constituencies according to how well disadvantaged children performed at different stages of their education, from early-years tests and school exams to entry into university and professional life.[13]

In England, as in America, where you live has a profound impact on your educational prospects. And the poorest districts are not necessarily the poorest performers. Two-thirds of teenagers in Bethnal Green and Bow in London are from low-income households. Yet they were almost four times as likely to get the national benchmark of five or more A*–C grades at GCSE as their peers living in Barnsley Central in South Yorkshire.[14]

Poorer pupils across the Midlands and North of England – in Derbyshire, Yorkshire and Nottinghamshire – were the least likely to do well. Education black spots included coastal towns, former industrial centres and many rural constituencies. On the other hand, London boasted thirty of the fifty best-performing areas, despite having high proportions of poor children.

Many of the constituencies represented by prominent political leaders performed poorly according to the Mobility Index. David Cameron's Witney constituency was ranked 475th out of 533, only slightly ahead of Labour leader Ed Miliband's Doncaster North, ranked 528th. The country's leaders seemed powerless to improve the prospects of the children they represented as Members of Parliament.

Some of least mobile districts in Britain achieved national notoriety. Knowsley in the north-west of England was found to have no A-level courses on offer for its teenagers.[15] Journalists revealed a community brutalized by ineffective education, deprivation and unemployment over successive generations. Children were growing up in families of 'trans-generational' unemployment where parents, grand-parents and even great-grandparents had never worked. Official census data revealed Knowsley's population to be 97 per cent white.

Cross Atlantic Parallels

The message from the first spatial study on income mobility across the United States resonates with the evidence on education and social mobility for Britain and elsewhere around the world.

The lowest opportunity districts in the United States are not necessarily the poorest areas of the country, but those with the biggest income gaps between rich and poor. Areas with larger Gini coefficients had smaller betas (less upward mobility). Chetty notes the link is 'consistent with the *Great Gatsby* curve documented across countries'. This does not prove that income gaps cause immobility, but just as Alan Krueger argued for country comparisons, the local patterns are exactly what you would expect if the relationship was causal.

High-opportunity areas were linked with higher test scores at local schools and lower drop-out rates for students. The research meanwhile confirms that family matters. One of the strongest factors linked with places of high opportunity in the US is a higher proportion of two-parent families. This again chimes with the international evidence. Children in Britain are at least twice as likely to have been born to teenage mothers as children in Australia and Canada.[16] And all this makes sense given the evidence in the early years suggesting stability aids the healthy development of young children. Yet little evidence exists of effective programmes or policies that could encourage such family stability. America's map of mobility appears to confirm that inequality, in all its economic and social dimensions, is linked with income mobility.

'Social capital indices', indicated by the strength of social networks and community involvement, were also significant. High upward mobility zones were populated with people more likely to participate in local civic organizations. These findings chime with those on America's 'social capital' divide presented by Robert Putnam.[17]

The Harvard academic has documented how the American professional classes are investing more in family life, community networks and civic activities. In contrast, supportive family life is fracturing among poorer and less educated families. Society's divide is not just economic but social, and this will likely limit future social mobility.[18]

The top echelons of society are pulling away from the bottom in myriad ways whether measured by school sport participation, obesity, maternal employment, single parenthood, financial stress or friendship networks. This gap amounts, Putnam fears, to a 'crisis' for the American dream. Taking the time to sit down with the family for dinner for Putnam is an 'indicator of the subtle but powerful investments that parents make in their kids (or fail to make)'.

In high-opportunity districts black and white and richer and poorer families were more likely to live side by side. One plausible theory for the higher levels of income mobility in Australia and Canada compared with Britain and the United

States is that, historically at least, they have experienced lower levels of social segregation in local communities.

Urban sprawl, as measured by commute times to work, on the other hand was bad for mobility: poor transport links limit access to job opportunities. The geographical isolation and poor transport links limiting the American dream in US cities has distinct echoes in the coastal communities left behind and stranded at the edges of England. Once prosperous seaside towns such as Blackpool, Lowestoft, Scarborough, Great Yarmouth, Hunstanton in Norfolk and Minehead in West Somerset have been identified as social mobility 'coldspots'. The demise of the tourist trade has been accentuated by poor transport links to England's main urban centres.[19]

These sad seaside towns are a reminder of the difficult question left unanswered by the Chetty work: it is all well and good to show people's lives are transformed by moving away from low-opportunity areas, but what about the communities left behind? While there is much merit in enabling talented young people from less privileged backgrounds to move out and move up the social ladder, this will have little impact on Britain's enduring stickiness at the bottom of society's ranks.

We must tread cautiously in drawing conclusions from America's Mobility Map, impressive as it is: these are features associated with high-opportunity areas, and not necessarily the causes of lower mobility. But for Chetty there is a positive message from the data: local policies can improve social mobility.

Political Divisions

The vote to leave the European Union in June 2016 prompted much reflection on the divisions it exposed across Britain. Growing regional education inequalities had contributed to the Brexit vote, claimed the Government's Chief Inspector of schools, Michael Wilshaw. Regions were in danger of adding a learning deficit to their economic one. 'If they sense that their children and young people are being denied the opportunities that exist elsewhere that will feed into the general sense that they are being neglected,' he argued. 'It wasn't just about leaving the European Union and immigration, it was the sense of disconnection with Westminster.'[20]

The vote was for some a 'two fingers' to the nation's political elites delivered by the socially immobile.[21] Younger voters who wanted to remain in the EU complained bitterly that the older generation, themselves the beneficiaries of the post-war boom in social mobility, had voted overwhelmingly for Brexit.

A survey carried out before the referendum had confirmed people's widespread pessimism about their prospects of climbing the social ladder.[22] Nearly 75 per cent believed it was difficult to move between classes, a rise from 65 per cent a decade previously. More than three out of four people thought the class divide was very or fairly wide. People believed British society is divided between a large disadvantaged group and a small privileged elite.

When Donald Trump was elected President of the United States in late 2016, Britain's social mobility tzar claimed there was an 'us and them' society on both sides of the Atlantic. Alan Milburn said there was a growing sense that 'a few unfairly hoard power and wealth', a situation that was 'deeply corrosive of our cohesion as a nation'. A survey found less than a third (29 per cent) of British people believed everyone in Britain has a fair chance to go as far as their talent and hard work will take them.[23]

For the US economist Lawrence Katz, one reason for the political unrest is that many people perceive that they no longer have a shot at a good local job in the way their parents did. There used to be a sense that you could get a job with a good employer in your town, even if you were not a college graduate, and it would lead to a long-term (and often unionized) job with reasonable benefits. 'It's the sense that there used to be a pathway, that if you worked hard you could get a good job and share in prosperity – if General Motors did well, you would do well. The sense that that pathway is gone has had a large political effect.'[24]

The backgrounds of those voting against the educated elites of Westminster and Washington were different in many ways, reflecting the countries' distinctive populations. But one common demographic group stood out: the white working class. Over two-thirds of white people without a college degree voted for Trump.[25] He was also backed by just under two-thirds of Americans who believed life would get worse for future generations. The least socially mobile areas of Britain meanwhile, many inhabited by white working-class communities, were those areas most likely to vote for Brexit. Trump said his rise to power was 'Brexit plus'.[26]

Our own analysis of the data confirms the link between

social mobility and voting patterns across the country at local authority level.[27] Brits with little chance of moving up tended to vote out. In South Derbyshire, six in ten people did so; in Barnsley, Normanton and Ashfield it was nearer seven in ten.[28] The people of Knowsley also voted to leave.

The first map in Figure 3.2 shows how the mobility prospects of those from disadvantaged backgrounds varies across local authorities in England; a darker shading reflects places with better mobility prospects and a 'colder' shade those with worse prospects. The second map shows the percentage of people voting to leave the European Union, with darker shades denoting a higher Leave vote and the lighter shades a higher remain vote. The two are close to being mirror images of each other. Where the first map shows more darkness, the second map shows less, and vice versa.

Social Mobility and Voting in the EU Referendum

The relationship between the Leave vote and the Social Mobility Commission's social mobility index for local authorities is shown in Figure 3.4. There is a strong link between areas of low mobility and areas that voted to leave the European Union. Each dot represents an area in England. Those on the left-hand side have the lowest mobility as measured by the index; those higher up on the graph had the largest majorities voting for Brexit. The straight 'best fit' line, calculated using all the data points, reveals the strong average association between the likelihood of voting for Brexit and levels of social mobility.

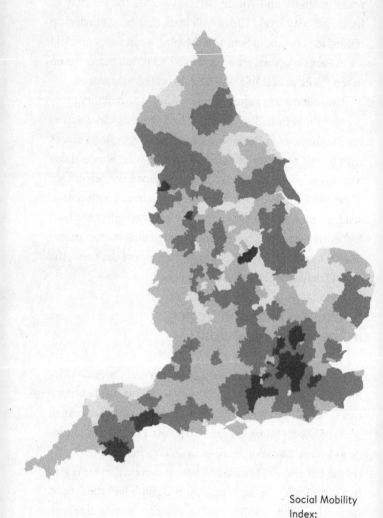

Social Mobility
Index:
-120 – -40
-40 – 0
0 – 40
40 – 120

Figure 3.2
Social mobility in england by local
authority.[29]

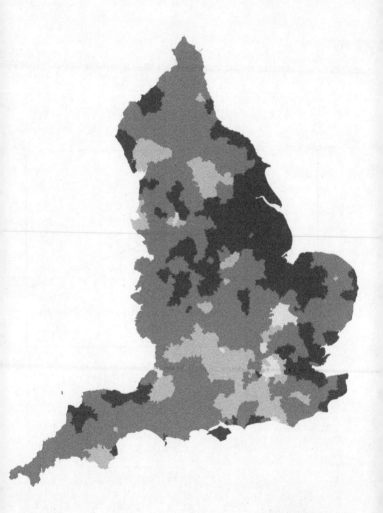

Figure 3.3
Leave voters in the EU referendum in England.

% Votes Leave:
20–40
40–50
50–60
60–80

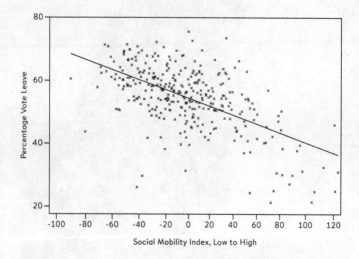

Figure 3.4
Brexit and social mobility in England's 320 local authorities.[30]

Our analysis of the voting data suggests the Leave campaign won the referendum partly because it persuaded the country's socially immobile that an independent Britain would hold better prospects for them – whether this was true or not. The Leave vote was strongest in areas of the country where people felt stuck in their lives and had lost confidence in the Government to change anything for the better.

The rhetoric from the elected leaders in both Britain and United States in 2016 played to the disaffected – promising to improve the lives of those failed by previous administrations. Prime Minister Theresa May vowed not to be driven by the interests of the privileged few, but by 'those of ordinary, working-class people'.[31] Trump meanwhile declared on the eve of his stunning electoral win that it would be a day that 'the American working class is going to strike back, finally'.[32]

Paradox of the American Dream

These high hopes will need to translate into policies that stand the test of time. Chetty's findings point to a paradox of the American Dream: the best places for upward mobility for the generation born in the 1980s were overwhelmingly the most expensive places to live for the millennial generation growing up in the early twenty-first century.[33] For young families seeking a better life for their children there is a limited window of opportunity. Timing as well as place matters.

San Jose in the 1980s had the perfect mix of factors that propelled many of its poorest residents into the upper echelons of America's earners: cheap housing, proximity to a burgeoning industry, and an integrated community including tightly knit immigrant communities. There are many theories as to why San Jose was such a hotbed of mobility: the city benefitted from the influx of highly aspirational Asian families as well as progressive local chief executives committed to pay workers in low-end jobs decent wages so they could live and function properly.

But by the early twenty-first century San Jose, in mobility terms at least, had become a victim of its own success. House prices skyrocketed to match the demand from highly paid employees in the booming businesses in Silicon Valley. The region's rich and poor increasingly lived in separate districts. Middle-earning jobs all but disappeared. Rents in San Jose grew by 42.6 per cent between 2006 and 2014.[34]

The same ominous pattern can be observed in London. The mix of aspirational communities, good schools and dynamic industries made the international metropolis a hotbed of social mobility. But escalating rents, exclusive school catchment areas and elite internships threaten to turn it into a coldspot of low opportunity.

In the intergenerational opportunity game, yesterday's high-mobility areas can be today's exclusive but stagnant communities. Schools become middle-class enclaves. Inequality in earnings balloons. Far from acting as the great social leveller, the education system is manipulated and taken over by elites and vested interests to ensure their offspring, irrespective of talent, do not slip down the social ladder.

PART TWO

Social Mobility and Education

CHAPTER 4

The Ever-Escalating Educational Arms Race

Education's Dark Side

The victors and victims of the education arms race are all around us: the tiger mums, super tutors and school-admission cheats. The foot soldiers are the weary children and their teachers, wilting under the unrelenting pressure to perform better each year. Even the winners in this race pay a heavy price for their apparent success.

Tanith Carey, a self-proclaimed tiger mum, has documented the damage done by hyper-competitive parenting to family life. Maximizing your children's talents is a full-time obsession: ferrying them from sports practice to musical renditions, scheduling tutoring sessions and extra classes over weekends. Tiger mums (and dads) are driven by a neurotic fear that no matter what they have done, it is never quite enough.

'Neurosis underpinned every conversation, as most of us had the same goal of getting our children into the same selective schools,' Carey told the *Daily Telegraph*. 'Then there was the depressing cloak-and-dagger secrecy and paranoia because we all lived with the constant fear that other mothers were doing more than we were.'[1] You can spot a tiger parent immediately: they inflate their child's achievements to anyone who will listen.

The Asian American academic Amy Chua first advocated a disciplinarian parenting style in her book *Battle Hymn of a Tiger Mother* (2011).[2] Grounded in East Asian culture, Chua's methods have spread to the West, lauded and loathed in equal measure. The British species is more panther-like, going to great lengths to conceal the extra coaching their children receive. The aim is to leave the impression that their sons and daughters are naturally brilliant. 'It's uncool to be a tiger mother,' Carey says. She claims to have tamed her tigerish instincts.[3]

There are no official estimates of tiger mum numbers in Britain. But we know there has been an explosion in private tutoring outside normal schooling hours. The percentage of children aged between 11 and 16 in England receiving private or home tuition rose by over a third in a decade, increasing from 18 per cent in 2005 to 25 per cent by 2016.[4] For teenagers in their GCSE years, the percentages are higher, reaching a third by 2016.

Within this upward trend, London has become the capital of private tuition: 42 per cent of young people in 2016 said they had received some form of tutoring, with tutors charging on average £29 an hour.[5] Conservative estimates put Britain's private tuition market at £1–2 billion a year.

The shadow education sector is a vast enterprise, purchased mostly by the elites. Pupils at private schools are twice as likely as state-educated pupils to receive private tuition.[6] Nearly half (43 per cent) of state school teachers had worked as private tutors outside the standard school day.

In this booming tuition industry, a new academic breed of supertutors are glorified as glamorous, globe-trotting

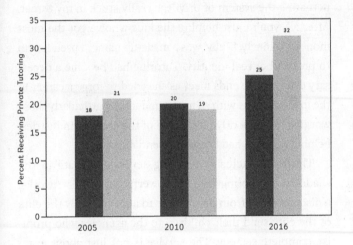

Figure 4.1
Private tutoring of secondary school children, 2005–2016.[7]

■ Years 7–11
■ Years 10–11

stars.[8] It's a life of teaching on yachts and planes, earning hundreds of pounds an hour. Yet it's also education's dark side. Oxbridge graduates are making a Faustian pact: serving the wealthy to pay their post-graduation debts.

'In my darker moments, I felt the only thing Oxford had prepared me for was to train other people to go to Oxford,' confided recent graduate Ruby Robson in one article. 'Perpetuating the system of privilege really stuck in my throat. After all, you're just helping the kids who've got the most money.' Tellingly, 'Ruby' was a made-up name, a pseudonym to protect her real identity. Tutoring had become a necessary evil to make ends meet as she tried to forge a career in the media.[9] But as with so many graduates, particularly those working in the poorly paid world of the creative industries, helping rich kids had become essential work.

The most exclusive tutoring services operate in the shadows, prospering through powerful personal networks: a discreet word from one banker to another. Only the elite of the elite send their children to the agencies who promise complete secrecy. The service is not just about exam results. Tutors will also equip children with the essential life skills needed to prosper in (and rule) the world – confidence, articulacy and resilience, as well as a certain charm. It is why overseas clients demand the most prestigious super tutor them of all: an Eton-educated Oxbridge graduate.[10]

The Great Social Leveller Myth

Many of us cling onto the hope that education can act as the great social leveller, enabling children from poorer backgrounds to overcome the circumstances they are born into. But evidence, gathered over a number of decades and for a range of countries, shows that for most children education has failed to live up to these expectations.

In no developed country for which we have data is there evidence that early-years centres, schools or colleges consistently reduce attainment gaps, and life prospects, between the rich and poor.[11] The education system at best acts as a counter-balance to the powerful forces outside the school gates driving bigger education gaps between the advantaged and disadvantaged.

The pattern observed is an ever-escalating educational arms race in which the poorest children are hopelessly ill-equipped to fight, and where the increasingly rich rewards go to the offspring of the social elites. Far from acting as a leveller, the education system has been exploited to retain advantage from one generation to the next. Individuals from wealthy backgrounds acquire higher qualifications that pave the way for higher earnings. Existing inequalities are transmitted and magnified across the generations. Social mobility falls.

The education system was expanded and upgraded with the aim of widening opportunities and developing talent from all backgrounds. Yet at every turn the privileged have found new ways to distinguish their offspring in the academic stakes.

In the past the middle-class advantage was found through A levels and university degrees; today it is achieved through postgraduate degrees and exclusive internships. A degree is no longer the automatic passport to a well-paid job it once was; now a particularly exclusive degree plus a master's qualification is required. Just as the education system expands to equalize opportunities, so a new frontier emerges enabling the well-off to climb one step up again.

The sociologist John Goldthorpe observes that 'parental – and, perhaps, grandparental – resources, even if not sufficient to allow for children to be educated in the private sector, are still widely deployed to buy houses in areas served by high-performing state schools, to pay for individual tutoring, to help manage student debt, to support entry into postgraduate courses for which no loans are available, or, in the case of educational failure, to fund "second chances".'[12]

With each passing generation the arms race becomes a more one-sided affair. Parents with more money and support are able to commandeer more powerful education weaponry for their offspring. Widening inequalities in income and inequalities in education reinforce each other in an endless feedback loop from one generation to the next.

In this race the biggest losers are the school leavers with no qualifications or skills at all. In recent decades, wage differentials between workers with more education and workers with less education have risen. An Oxbridge degree confers a much bigger advantage than a 'bog standard' degree. Failing to get basic GCSEs at age 16 incurs a bigger penalty in working life than for previous generations. It is why those leaving school without basic numeracy and literacy skills – the lost souls we describe in the next chapter – are at an increasing disadvantage.

The signs of this arms race are all around us: tiger parents, super tutors, escalating levels of private tuition and private school fees, and inflated house prices in the neighbourhoods of the most sought-after state schools.

Sharp-elbowed Warriors

Some of the fiercest battles are fought at the gates of sought-after schools. Oversubscribed schools select children using a range of criteria: how near they live to the school, how much they have attended a particular local church, or how well they do in academic entrance tests. Whatever the method, the result is the same: too many anxious parents fighting over limited places. And the winners are the off-spring of the sharp-elbowed chattering classes.

'Nothing causes parents, particularly middle-class parents, so much angst as secondary school admissions. Drugs, crime, underage sex, foul language, truancy, rap music, acne and smart answers, plus exam results that don't allow entry to a decent university – all these, it is feared, are the potential results of a bad secondary school,' observed the journalist Peter Wilby.[13] 'Go to a dinner party in Islington or Edgbaston, and they will talk of little else.'

One way to get ahead is to pay the inflated prices of houses in the vicinity of the 'best' schools. Poorer pupils have been priced out of the catchment areas of popular comprehensives in England because local houses cost £45,700 more than elsewhere.[14] Meanwhile a school at the top of the education rankings attracts a house price premium of around 12 per cent relative to a school ranked at the bottom.[15]

It is an investment worth making. Paying for a good education by taking out a mortgage is a cheaper option than paying the fees for a private school if you have two children (and much the same deal for one). The children's improved results make it a sound investment. Researchers concluded school selection by mortgage 'reinforces school segregation and inequalities in performance and achievement, and reduces social mobility across the generations'.[16]

Surveys of parents confirm these middle-class manoeuvres. One in three (32 per cent) professional parents with school-aged children had moved to an area they thought had good schools, while one in five (18 per cent) had moved to the catchment area of a specific school.[17] Those from higher social classes are more likely to deploy strategies that cost money, including moving home or hiring a private tutor to help their children. A significant minority of parents admitted to cheating in school admissions: buying a second home, or renting a property nearby. These admissions over admissions are likely to be the tip of the iceberg.

Such underhand tactics explode the illusion of an orderly and respectful British society where everyone plays by the rules. Much to everyone's embarrassment, admissions cheats are occasionally outed into full public glare. 'You are doing poor kids out of school places and homes. You are making local schools selective on income by the back door,' complained the journalist Giles Coren, in his column for *The Times*. 'You are destroying the very notion of a local school by coring out catchment areas and then abandoning them.' Coren was attacking his 'lying, cheating, hypocritical' new neighbours.[18] His daughter Kitty had failed to get a place at her local outstanding primary school, just 200 yards away from the home where Coren had lived for twenty years. Sharp-elbowed parents had exploited a loophole in the admissions rules by renting a place nearer the school, pretending this was their permanent home. Teachers had only noticed the scam when a stream of new families notified the school office of 'a change in home address' soon after their children had started at the school. 'It is very well known that this is going on,' one peeved parent told the local newspaper.[19]

Council officials vowed to tackle 'abuses' of the school admissions system and to investigate 'fraud' where parents were being dishonest, tightening up its rules to not accept temporary addresses. But the middle classes had already identified a new deceit: paying private doctors to provide evidence for 'exceptional medical or social reasons' to catapult their children to the front of the school queue. Ailments, just like addresses, could mysteriously disappear once term had begun. Coren's daughter ended up leaving the state system and going to a private school. The real losers, he acknowledged, were children from poorer homes who had been pushed out of their local school and had no other option but to attend a state school much further away. Like many aspects of the education arms race, it seems school admissions are just not fair.

An Early Start: The 'Rug Rat Race'

The academic race is over for many children when they have barely started primary school. For his PhD project Leon Feinstein was interested in the earliest education trajectories of children growing up in Britain: how do the gaps in cognitive development widen between poorer children and their more privileged peers? He summarized his findings in one simple and now famous graph, reproduced in Figure 4.2.[20]

Feinstein's 'crossover' graph charts the trajectories of children with known levels of initial achievement at 22 months, indicated by their scores in standard psychological tests. It shows how strongly their subsequent development depends on their socio-economic status (SES). High-SES children who started with low levels of achievement overcome their early difficulties by mid-childhood; their high-SES counterparts who started as high-performers maintain their position in tests at age ten. The opposite holds true for low-SES children. Initial low-performers remain rooted at the bottom of the class as they grow older; initial high-performers from similarly poor (low-SES) backgrounds fall back down to the average by age ten.

The *Guardian* journalist Polly Toynbee put it more baldly, contrasting the trajectories of the bright child from a poor home and 'a dim but rich baby': 'The two children are already on a steep trajectory in opposite directions: the poor/bright one travelling fast downwards; the rich/dim one moving up, as their social backgrounds counteract their inborn abilities.'[21]

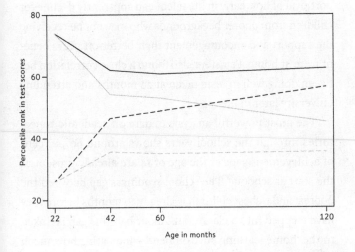

Figure 4.2

Cognitive development of young children and their parents'
socio-economic status.

——— High SES, high ability

- - - High SES, low ability

——— Low SES, high ability

- - - Low SES, low ability

Other researchers have questioned the reliability of test scores undertaken by children as early as age two, suggesting these patterns may reflect the 'regression to the mean' effect that sees many characteristics naturally drift back to their average value.[22] But Feinstein's graph remains a powerful portrayal of how early in life talent can apparently decline for children from poorer backgrounds who may not be receiving the support and encouragement their better-off peers benefit from at home. Feinstein also found a close correlation between doing well in tests taken at 22 months and attending university later in life.

The most powerful analysis to date on academic trajectories through the school years shows around 60 per cent of achievement gaps at the age of 14 are already present at the start at school.[23] The school-readiness gap between the poorest and richest children is already 19 months before they have stepped into a classroom. About half this gap is linked to the 'home learning environment' – indicating how much parents support the learning of their children.

Britain, alongside the US, also has an education gap between poorer children and their richer peers that widens as children age. In the UK this widening occurs at age 11, at the start of secondary school. The link between family income and test scores is found to be strongest in the UK, signalling that levels of educational inequality are higher than in more socially mobile countries.[24]

The evidence also suggests those from poorer backgrounds have to work harder to compete and get the same academic grades as their more privileged peers. The link between earlier cognitive tests and exam performance weakened for children born in 1970 compared with those born in 1958. This suggests school tests are as much a signal of how much support children receive as their natural ability. Although researchers point out that cognitive tests taken at younger ages are themselves the product of the environments shaping children in their early years.[25] Untapped academic potential is likely to be one of the reasons why state school pupils with similar A levels are more likely than their equally qualified private school peers to secure top degrees at university.

The firing gun of the educational arms race begins well before children's first day at school: whatever solutions we have for improving social mobility will need to act outside as well as inside the school gates and before school has even started. There are parallels with the patterns observed in the United States. American economists have come up with a term for the extra investments made by middle-class families to enable their children to get ahead during the early years: the 'the rug rat race'.[26]

Higher Frontiers

As Winston Churchill's former wartime economic adviser, Lionel Robbins was used to fighting his corner. But when Prime Minister Harold Macmillan tasked the economist with looking into expanding the country's universities in 1961, he came up against unexpected opposition. An enraged representative of the Left-leaning Association of University Teachers claimed universities were 'already scraping the barrel'; any more people allowed in would damage academic standards.[27] The prospect of more degrees 'would be absolutely appalling'. If this was the reaction from the trade unionists responding to the Labour Party's own parallel inquiry, one can only imagine the social snobbery expressed elsewhere.

Lord Robbins waved away the objections. He was convinced the country needed graduates from all backgrounds to supply an expanding professional workforce. IQ tests demonstrated that young people from working-class homes were intellectually capable, despite performing badly in their 11-plus examinations. His final report established the 'Robbins principle': this declared university places 'should be available to all who are qualified by ability and attainment to pursue them and who wish to do so'. This aspiration has remained at the heart of higher education policy ever since.

Yet following the Second World War, the slow march of Britain's universities from a tiny elite to an expanded higher education system remained a highly exclusive endeavour. In 1940, 50,000 students attended a small clutch of institutions including the ancient seats of learning, Oxford and Cambridge. Just 1.5 per cent of 18–19 year olds from working-class groups enrolled on degree courses in 1940 compared with 8.4 per cent from the professional classes; in 1990 the equivalent figures were 10 per cent and 37 per cent. It took fifty years before the proportion of working-class students surpassed the enrolment rate of their more privileged counterparts in 1940. And by that time the university access gap had widened.[28]

The next three decades experienced the mad rush to a mass higher education system. Few countries in the world have expanded universities at such breakneck speed. In Figure 4.3 we document the growth using our own data. In 1980, 9 per cent of 26–30-year-olds were university graduates; by 2015, 39 per cent of 26–30-year-olds had a degree. The official figures show there were over 2.2 million young full-time students enrolled at British universities.[29]

For all this expansion, our analysis of the data reveals that the graduation gap between rich and poor has widened. Figure 4.4 records the percentage of young people who graduate from university by age 23, comparing those from the poorest fifth of families with those from the richest fifth. The proportion of young people from the poorest fifth of homes graduating from university increased by 12 percentage points between 1981 and 2013, growing from 6 to 18 per cent over the period. The graduation rate for young people from the richest fifth of homes meanwhile went up from 20 per cent to 55 per cent. Nearly twenty-five years on, the graduation rate for those from the poorest families has still to exceed the rate for those from the richest families in 1981.

Robbins's vision of a university system accessible to all has yet to materialize. A study tracking the entry (rather than graduation) rates on to university degrees from the mid-1990s until 2011–12 suggested the enrolment gap at least had begun to narrow.[30] But the bad news was that it had widened at the country's most prestigious universities. The participation of the most advantaged fifth of young people at highly selective universities rose from 15.4 per cent to 18.1 per cent during the period. The participation of the most disadvantaged two-fifths of young people in contrast rose by just half a percentage point, from 2.4 per cent to 2.9 per cent. By 2011,

	1980	1990	2000	2010	2017
Some Qualifications	64	81	91	93	95
A-Levels or Higher	30	40	38	55	62
Degree	9	12	20	31	38
Postgraduate Degree	1	1	5	10	11

Figure 4.3
Highest educational qualification:
percentage of 26–30-year-olds.[31]

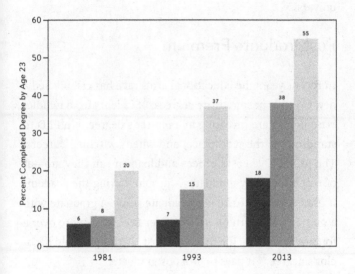

Figure 4.4
Educational inequality, 1981 to 2013.[32]

■ Age 16: Lowest 20% family income
■ Age 16: Middle 60% family income
■ Age 16: Highest 20% family income

the most advantaged fifth of young people were 6.3 times more likely to enter one of the elite universities.

In the ever-escalating educational race, the middle classes had clocked that a bog standard degree no longer counted enough; now what was required to distinguish yourself from the rest of the pack was an elite degree from a prestigious university.

Postgraduate Premium

In recent years the educational arms race has established a new frontier: postgraduate degrees.[33] Students from middle-class homes are investing in a master's degree or a PhD to stand out in the workplace, and when switching careers. The prohibitive costs of fees and loans mean they are out of reach for many graduates – despite having the academic grades to undertake postgraduate study. A graduate with a master's will earn on average over £200,000 more over a forty-year working life than a graduate with a plain old bachelor's degree.[34] It pays to be a postgraduate.

In 1996, just 1 per cent of 26–60-year-olds in the workforce held a postgraduate degree; in 2015 this had risen to 13 per cent. Over 2 million working adults had a master's degree or PhD. But this 'educational upgrading' was generated almost exclusively by extra numbers of postgraduates from the richest homes.

In 1991, 2 per cent of 23-year-olds from the poorest fifth of homes had postgraduate degrees compared with 8 per cent from the richest fifth of homes – a gap of 6 per cent. In 2004, 3 per cent of 24-year-olds from the poorest fifth of homes had postgraduate degrees compared with 13 per cent from the richest fifth of homes – a gap of 10 per cent. Inequality in postgraduate education had nearly doubled in thirteen years.[35]

Paying Education's Price

Perennial scare stories of graduates having to settle for low-paid work remain unfounded. A good degree remains a smart investment. The wage returns for degrees have held up remarkably well despite the bulging numbers of graduates now competing for jobs.[36] The opposite side of the coin is an increasingly high penalty for not going on to higher education and for leaving school without qualifications.

The education haves and have-nots are creating the earnings haves and have-nots, one of the reasons why labour market inequality has become higher in Britain. What jobs people get and how much they earn after they finish their education is often the forgotten half of the social mobility equation. Policy makers are caught by the allure of trying to address educational inequalities. Yet any successful efforts to improve social mobility levels are likely to have to narrow gaps both in education and in the workplace.

Economists have charted how technological advances are making many middle-tier jobs redundant – the so-called hollowing out of the labour market.[37] In the knowledge-based economy, a university education will matter even more. Not only this, many new jobs in the future will require the essential life skills – articulacy, resilience, confidence and people skills – which the right education helps to nurture.[38]

Our own analysis of the latest data from the Labour Force Survey reveals a significant and growing wage premium for graduates compared to people without degrees. In 1980, male graduates earned on average 46 per cent more than their non-graduate counterparts. In 2017 this earnings uplift was 66 per cent. This continuing advantage from higher study was by no means a certainty given the growing numbers of graduates.

Figure 4.5 documents the differences in wages for increasing levels of education for successive generations. Wage returns for degrees (compared to just having school qualifications) have held up: graduates remain highly valued in the workplace. At the same time the average relative wage boost for having a degree has declined for the most recent generations. This is a sign of the increasing variation of the wage returns for different types of degrees.

The wage returns from gaining a postgraduate degree (compared with just having an undergraduate degree) have continued to rise. A master's degree is now equivalent to what a plain university degree meant a few generations ago. It is no surprise that some academic research has pitched postgraduate education as 'the new frontier of social mobility'.[39]

Sociologists have depicted this as more of a rearguard action by the middle classes: 'defensive expenditure' aimed at preserving their children's competitive edge. Parents are aware education, in relation to employment, operates primarily as a 'positional good', argues John Goldthorpe. What matters is not how much education you acquire but how

	1980	1990	2000	2010	2017
A-Levels v. less than A-Levels	6	26	31	25	23
Undergraduate degree v. A-Levels	28	28	21	19	13
Postgraduate degree v. Undergraduate degree	3	-3	6	9	15

Figure 4.5
Wage differentials by highest education qualification,
26–30-year-olds.[40]

much more and superior education you acquire compared with others you are competing with in the jobs market.[41]

Variation That Lies Beneath

These average figures conceal increasing variation in the earnings returns to different types of degrees – distinctions middle-class parents are acutely aware of. With more graduates in the jobs market, employers have become more discerning: it matters which subject you studied your degree in and at which university.

The most detailed picture yet of the variations in graduate earnings has been produced by researchers from the Institute of Fiscal Studies and Cambridge and Harvard universities. They studied English graduates a decade after finishing their degrees, using tax and student loan records. More than 10 per cent of male graduates from the London School of Economics, Oxford and Cambridge were already earning more than £100,000 in the tax year 2012–13. But the median earnings of graduates from some universities were less than those for non-graduates. Overall median earnings for male graduates ten years after graduation were found to be £30,000, compared with £21,000 for non-graduates. Non-graduates were twice as likely to have no earnings at all.

Subjects such as medicine, economics, law, maths and business delivered substantial wage premiums compared with typical graduates. The creative arts produced earnings more typical of non-graduates. These variations in earnings were attributable to other factors over and above the differences in student intakes to begin with. Students with higher A-level grades and higher earning potential would be expected to enrol onto highly selective degree courses. But this study demonstrated that the university degree you take does make an extra difference to your future wage packet.

Most disturbingly from a social mobility perspective, universities fail to level the playing field. Graduates from richer family backgrounds were found to earn 10 per cent more after graduation than their poorer counterparts. This was the case even though they had completed the same degrees at the same universities. The gap doubled for the highest earners.[42]

The Baffling World of University Admissions

The small gains in numbers of disadvantaged students enrolling at universities have come despite the introduction of university fees in England of £9,000 a year. Graduates pay back Government loans when they start earning a decent salary – £25,000 a year.[43] But the extra charges for degrees, required to fund the continuing expansion of universities, have coincided with a worrying fall in numbers of part-time and mature students.[44]

Fears over fees remain. A Government report revealed a falling proportion of state-educated students entering higher education in the year the £9,000 fees were introduced.[45] This was in contrast to their privately educated counterparts, prompting renewed concerns that the higher fees (and the replacement of maintenance grants with student loans) will be detrimental to social mobility. Students across the UK also have to grapple with the complexity of different fees, loans and grants systems in England, Scotland, Wales and Northern Ireland. In England moreover the student finance system is prone to constant Government tampering and review.[46]

But these debates have overshadowed what is arguably a bigger concern: poorer students investing in degree courses with low or even negative returns in earnings. In the educational arms race this is harming your prospects through self-inflicted wounds. For first-generation students without the tacit knowledge of the middle classes, choosing the right degree has become one of life's most important investment decisions – at a time when the market is increasingly complex and confusing.

Quite apart from the dizzying array of bursaries, scholarships and fee remissions on offer for 50,000-plus degree courses,[47] and information on the likely employment prospects they may lead to,[48] there are an array of admissions criteria deployed by universities as they try to distinguish between equally well-qualified candidates. These include personal statements, teacher recommendations, school exam grades, university admissions tests, interviews, 'contextual offers' and much more.[49]

At Oxford and Cambridge, the most sought-after of all the academic elites, this complexity goes to new levels: the applications and admissions process involves earlier deadlines, interviews with specialist tutors at one of the sixty-nine independent colleges (with their own preferences and traditions) that make up the universities, as well as an increasing battery of bespoke subject tests.[50]

There is evidence that talented students in state schools suffer from the 'not the likes of me' attitude which precludes them from applying to the most prestigious universities in the first place.[51] This can be made worse by well-meaning but risk-averse teachers.[52]

An analysis of personal statements, intended for students to sell themselves to prospective universities, revealed a chasm in quality and style between independent and state school applicants.[53] Independent school applicants were more likely to have well-written statements, with fewer grammatical errors, 'filled with high-status and relevant activities'. One privately educated 18-year-old shared how they had been working 'for a designer in London; as a model; on the trading floor of a London broker's firm; with my local BBC radio station; events planning with a corporate five-star country hotel; in the marketing team of a leading City law firm . . . and most recently managing a small gastro pub'. This was contrasted with statements from state school pupils who struggled to draw on suitable work and life experiences.

Good quality information, advice and guidance for school pupils are essential in such a complex world of admissions. Yet the research suggests at least half of the advice currently given in schools is inadequate, and can be poorly timed and partial.[54] If you ever wanted to create a higher education system that acts to confuse, baffle and alienate the non-privileged outsiders trying to get a good education and a foothold on life's income ladder, then this surely is it.

At the same time it is widely acknowledged that we have failed to create a viable alternative route of 'vocational' apprenticeships that for many young people could offer a better option for their life prospects. It is as if the other half of young people pursuing non-academic routes do not exist. While there are still far too few advanced apprenticeships on offer, it is little known that they can lead to greater earning returns than many degrees.[55]

Battles in Later Life

There is another emerging battleground in the arms race: who secures internships during the early critical stages of careers after university study is over. Increasingly internships are the key gateways to starting a professional career. Unpaid and often unadvertised, these positions have become yet another impediment to social mobility.[56]

The impact of coming from a less privileged background continues long after education has finished. Britain's social mobility challenge is far from over once the graduation ceremonies are concluded. International comparative studies suggest this is a particular issue for Britain. Gaining a good education appears to genuinely equalize life prospects in the United States, but only has limited power in this country.[57]

Sociologists have identified a 'class ceiling' in Britain preventing the upwardly mobile from enjoying equivalent earnings to those from upper-middle-class backgrounds. Analysing the 2014 Labour Force Survey, the researchers investigated the earnings of people in elite occupations, comparing how income varies by social-class background.

People in elite occupations whose parents were employed in semi-routine and routine working-class jobs ('the long-range upwardly mobile') earn on average £6,200 a year less than their colleagues from higher professional and managerial backgrounds ('the intergenerationally stable'). This was the case even after taking into account a host of factors including educational qualifications, job tenure, the 'London effect', ethnicity, gender, age, hours worked, firm size, and whether a person worked in the public or private sector.

There was striking variation across different elite occupations. At one end of the scale, engineering provided a notable exemplar of meritocracy, with negligible differences in pay regardless of social background. In contrast, the children of the working classes experienced a particularly large pay disadvantage in law, media, medicine and finance.

The researchers concluded: 'There is no . . . easy distinction between "the person you were born" and "the person you become". As our results show, individuals tend to always carry – at least in some shape or form – the symbolic baggage of the past. Moreover, the imprint of this history can have important consequences for both how people act in the present, and – perhaps more importantly – how they are evaluated by others.'[58]

Superior Life Skills

Sociologists confirm that privileged children in Britain who fail to make the mark academically avoid the knock to their life prospects that children from poorer backgrounds experience. This is due in part to the 'social capital' gained from their middle-class upbringing, conclude the researchers, equipping such children with the social skills ideally suited to the growing number of service and sales jobs in the economy: 'In addition perhaps to helpful social networks, are the – very marketable – "soft skills" and lifestyle and personal characteristics that these individuals acquire, less through their education than through their family, community and peer-group socialization.'[59]

There is growing evidence that accumulating essential life skills as well as social and cultural capital is instrumental to future life prospects. These are the 'non-academic' attributes as well as the tacit knowledge to get by in middle-class circles. The inexorable rise of A grades and first-class degrees has ironically put an extra premium on the non-academic characteristics that distinguish some candidates from the rest. You need not only to pass the grade, but to exhibit the right behaviours to succeed. As we have seen, these other attributes, whether social, cultural on financial, may partly account for privately educated students being more likely to enter top occupations and elite universities than their similarly academically qualified state school peers.

The so-called 'brown shoes effect' summarized how young people from less privileged backgrounds lost out on banking jobs because of their dress, accent and behaviour. Investment banks were turning away talented youngsters from poorer backgrounds as they simply did not fit in with expected cultural norms, including dress codes. The wearing of brown shoes with a business suit was a faux pas too far.[60]

Middle-class parents are acutely attuned to the importance of social as well as academic skills in the educational arms race. Much of the evidence gathered on 'enrichment gaps' in the United States resonates with the trends observed in Britain. It suggests an increasingly wide divide. The richest families in the US spent seven times more on out-of-school cultural enrichment (including for example museum visits) than the poorest families, a much bigger gap than forty years previously. The Harvard academic Robert Putnam has documented how the American professional classes are investing more in family life, community networks and civic activities.[61]

Surveys in Britain have also revealed significant gaps in the extra-curricular enrichment children are exposed to.[62] Inequalities in the essential life skills of children emerge early.[63] Children from poorer homes tend to exhibit, on average, worse self-control (conduct) and emotional health than their wealthier peers. These differences are apparent for children aged three years old. The gap in essential life skills between poorer children and everyone else has widened over the past thirty years.[64]

In this race, it is difficult to distinguish between working the system and stepping over the line. Research for the BBC found one in five students in private schools had received extra time to complete examinations – compared with one in eight pupils in state schools.[65] Private school heads were accused of gaming the exam system to boost their results. Yet they could just be doing a good job of identifying students with genuine special educational needs.

In a separate incident, a Government inquiry was launched to investigate accusations that teachers at Eton and other leading public schools had passed information to pupils about their upcoming exams. The scandal prompted resignations at the schools and calls for tighter rules under which teachers work as examiners writing and reviewing question papers. Announcing the inquiry, the Schools Minister Nick Gibb warned: 'cheating of any kind is unacceptable.'[66]

The education system remains tilted in countless ways to the already advantaged. Glass floors limit downward mobility of those from privileged backgrounds and class ceilings limit upward mobility of those who happen to be born into poorer homes. Whether by foul means or fair, the escalating educational arms race is far from a level playing field.

CHAPTER 5

Education's Lost Souls

High Illiteracy in the Developed World

At various times the Organization for Economic Co-operation and Development (OECD) has surveyed thousands of adults across the world to assess their basic skills. Survey questions attempt to assess people's ability to solve everyday 'real world' problems. In 2012 the basic numeracy question in Figure 5.1 was posed to 16–65-year-olds.[1]

While thinking about the answer, consider a much more surprising statistic. A quarter of British adults got the answer wrong. And the proportion answering incorrectly was the same for those aged under and over 30. (The answer, by the way, is 36 litres.) The same proportion failed the questions on basic literacy. The shocking results prompted the OECD to label British youngsters the 'most illiterate in the developed world'.[2]

Mastering maths and English is the most basic requirement for prospering in life. People with improved literacy and numeracy skills are more likely to be employed.[3] And in England, this link is particularly strong; not only this, people with stronger literacy and numeracy tend to be more healthy.[4]

Our own analysis of the OECD data from its Programme for the International Assessment of Adult Competencies

Figure 5.1
Sample question in the OECD Basic Numeracy Test, 2012.
'Look at the petrol gauge image. The petrol tank holds 48 litres.
How many litres remain in the tank?'

(PIAAC), an international survey of adult skills in twenty-four countries, is presented in Figure 5.2. Adults were assessed as having one of five proficiency levels in basic skills. People at Level 1 have low skills: they are unable to digest basic figures and words; they find it difficult understanding pay slips or household bills, or working out a household budget. People at Level 3 are secure in the skills that enable them to function perfectly well in everyday life – roughly equivalent to gaining good GCSEs or even A levels at secondary school.

A quarter of 16–65-year-olds in England were found to have substandard numeracy skills: they scored at Level 1 or below. Moreover – and unlike in other countries – the position was the same for 16–29 and 30–65-year-olds in 2012. This extrapolates to around 10 million unskilled adults across Britain. Separate Government surveys have confirmed these alarming patterns, finding the proportion of 16–18-year-olds without basic numeracy skills had gone up from 21 per cent in 2003 to 28 per cent in 2011.[5]

International Comparisons

England's rising illiteracy and innumeracy levels contrast with smaller and declining proportions of younger people with low skills in other countries (Canada, Finland, the Netherlands and the United States) as Figure 5.3 shows. Only the United States has a higher proportion of adults missing basic numeracy skills. Canada, which has high income mobility levels, lies in between the better performing Finland and the Netherlands and the worse performing England and United States.

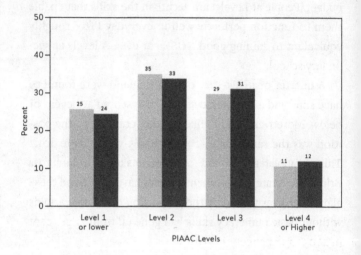

Figure 5.2
Numeracy levels by age: England.[6]

Aged 16–29
Aged 30–65

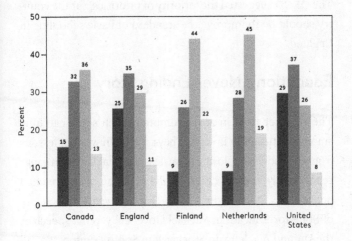

Figure 5.3
Numeracy levels, 16–29-year-olds, by country.[7]

■ Level 1 or lower
■ Level 2
■ Level 3
■ Level 4 or higher

The message from these data is sobering. England is losing the international race in basic skills. The position is reasonably good at the top end of the skills distribution, but dire at the bottom. And the figures throw some doubt over the standards of our higher education system. Even one in ten university graduates were classified as having low skills. The OECD suggested the 'priority of priorities' for the country should be to improve the standard of basic schooling in England.[8]

Education's Never-Ending Story

The summer riots in 2011 prompted much soul-searching among politicians in Britain.[9] They tried to draw wider lessons from the sudden explosion of lawlessness that had seen gangs roam openly in inner cities, battling with an over-stretched police force. In the anxious weeks that followed, the Secretary of State for Education, Michael Gove, delivered a speech at the Durand Academy in Stockwell in South London. 'For all the advances we have made, and are making in education, we still, every year allow thousands more children to join an educational underclass – they are the lost souls our school system has failed,' he told an invited audience.[10]

Primary school teachers had spoken about the growing difficulty they faced with children who arrived unprepared to learn. A growing number of children were unable to form letters or even hold a pencil. Many could not sit and listen during lessons. Others could barely speak a full sentence of proper words, let alone frame a question.

When they arrived at secondary school these children

were still unable to read or write, often covering up their deficiencies by acting tough and disrupting lessons. Many ended up being placed in 'Alternative Provision' or 'Pupil Referral Units'. Despite the heroic efforts of teachers, the destiny of these pupils was all too predictable: they would become the next generation of street gangs and prison inmates. They faced a world of multidimensional poverty – 'a poverty of ambition, a poverty of discipline, a poverty of soul'.

Durand was one of the new 'academy' schools that were the Coalition Government's flagship policy.[11] In Gove's eyes it was exactly the type of school that would address low levels of literacy and numeracy. Yet within three years, Gove had been removed as Education Secretary.[12] And in 2016 the Department for Education announced that it was withdrawing funds from the Durand Academy Trust following 'serious concerns about financial management and governance'.[13] Meanwhile another cohort of children would leave school lacking basic literacy and numeracy skills.

Ineffectual Education Reforms

The uncomfortable truth is that Gove's 'underclass' of illiterate and innumerate pupils has remained immune to countless education reforms ushered in by successive governments. Policy has swung from market-based reforms to highly prescribed edicts on what teachers should do. School funding has been increased (and then cut). Targets have been set (and then re-cast). Commitments have been made (and then discarded). Yet the numbers of young people without the most basic skills remain as high as ever.

The 1988 Education Reform Act ushered in the publication of school league tables and school inspections, and a national curriculum. But for all these reforms, pupils in the bottom tenth of the class saw their grades deteriorate over the period.[14]

Before the 1997 general election, Tony Blair presented a sobering analysis of the performance of the country's school system. 'We have a major problem at the bottom', he said.[15] A blizzard of education initiatives followed, aiming to close the gap between poorer children and their more privileged peers, underpinned by a big increase in funding for schools.[16] It signalled a sea change in education policy, combining market policies and state interventions – the so-called 'third way'.

These policies ranged from help for schools in urban areas such as the London Challenge, to nationally prescribed 'literacy hours' and 'numeracy hours' for primary schools.[17] Academies – schools independent of local authority control – were created to take over struggling schools.[18] But by most measures there was only a tiny reduction in the overall attainment gap between the poorest pupils and other pupils during 1997–2010.[19] In 2010 seven in every ten children (68.8 per cent) on free school meals failed to secure the national expectation of five grades of C or more, including English and maths, in their GCSEs at age 16.[20] Labour's record had been disappointing.[21]

The proportion of young people aged 16–18 who were not in education, employment and training (so-called NEETs) also failed to reduce under Labour's watch, 'indicating that a persistent minority of young people remained disaffected with school, achieving little and facing very poor post-school prospects'.[22]

Coalition Reforms

In 2010 it was the new Coalition Government's turn to cite the country's poor performance internationally.[23] Its flagship social mobility policy was £2.5 billion of 'Pupil Premium' funds every year for children qualifying for free school meals.[24] The Pupil Premium was one of a host of major changes. These included a new national curriculum, traditional end-of-year tests and more academies.[25] Education policy would lurch back to the laissez-faire market policies of the 1980s.

Against this backdrop of change, a movement to introduce evidence-led practices emerged. The Sutton Trust published a 'pupil premium toolkit' to help schools spend funds on 'best bets' according to research on what had worked in the classroom.[26] The Education Endowment Foundation was established to evaluate effective approaches for improving the results of the poorest pupils.[27]

But the achievement gap between poorer children and their better-off peers was wider than previously assumed. Driven by the pressure to rank highly in published league tables, schools had encouraged their poorest pupils to take vocational qualifications of dubious quality. This helped to boost the standing of a school, since these qualifications enabled them to record more pupils reaching expected benchmarks. Yet the truth was that most of the qualifications had little benefit for the children themselves.[28] In 2014 teenagers on free school meals fell further behind their more privileged peers. Two-thirds failed to achieve five GCSEs with at least C grades including English and maths.[29]

Reviews of progress on narrowing the gap have adopted an increasingly despairing tone. One report concluded there was 'currently no prospect' of the gap being eliminated at secondary school – despite billions of pounds being targeted on the poorest pupils.[30] Another estimated that, based on the most optimistic assumptions, it would take another fifty years to reach an equitable school system.[31]

Basic Skill Gaps

In 2011 a Government report laid bare the extent of the basic skills problem facing the country. The Wolf review, commissioned to overhaul vocational qualifications, found that obtaining at least a grade C in English and Maths GCSEs had become the new universal entry requirement for employers, sixth-form colleges and universities. Just short of half of all students had failed to achieve a C grade in GCSE in English or maths by age 16; at age 18 the figure was still below 50 per cent. Over 300,000 pupils had failed to master the basics in maths or English. 'These are shocking figures,' said Alison Wolf, an economist from King's College London.[32]

Teenagers were forced to do re-sits in English and maths – many in poorly funded further education colleges. But in 2016 only 29.5 per cent of 17-year-olds (and older) subsequently achieved their grade C in maths; and 26.9 per cent in English.[33] The majority of students failing to make the mark yet again were doubtless the same illiterates and innumerates highlighted by the OECD.

To understand how a 16- or 17-year-old can leave education without basic skills, you need look no further than a school register detailing the tough lives of their most troubled pupils. These are deeply harrowing tales involving years of instability, abuse and violence at home as young children. Multiple dimensions of disadvantage build up through the childhood years and have a cumulative impact, leaving few prospects of upward social mobility for these young people.

Their upbringing manifests itself in many ways. If they do attend school, they are unable to control their emotions, with frequent outbursts of anger. They are prone to impulsive behaviour and low moods, and have few friends. Often they are moved from one school to the next. They are at risk of drug addiction and involvement in gangs.[34]

These testimonies tally with the characteristics revealed from surveys of adult skills. Unskilled adults have relatively poor physical health and mental wellbeing; and they are more likely to receive state benefits.[35] They made up half of the 2 million people unemployed in England in 2012.[36]

The Problem That Can Only Get Worse

The problem of the low-skilled losers of the education system is set to magnify for future generations. The crippling disability of low skills is passed down from one generation to the next. Our own analysis of the OECD data is summarized in Figure 5.4, showing the proportion of adults with low numeracy skills for the under- and over-30s in England, but now broken down by their parents' education levels. Over 60 per cent of the under-30s whose parents had failed to gain secondary school qualifications (admittedly by 2012 a relatively small fraction) had lower numeracy skills. This

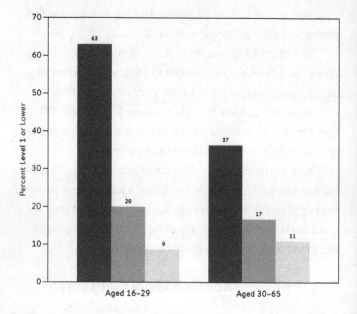

Figure 5.4
Numeracy Level 1 or lower in England, by age and parental education.[37]

■ Neither parent has upper secondary education
■ At least one parent has upper secondary education
■ At least one parent has tertiary education

contrasts with the 9 per cent of the same age group who had at least one graduate parent. The intergenerational persistence of substandard education and skills is much stronger for the under-thirties than for the over-thirties.

These results chime with many others. The link between parental background and adult skills among 16- to 24-year-olds was found to be stronger in England than in all other countries except the Slovak Republic.[38] Meanwhile children whose parents had the poorest numeracy skills were twice as likely to perform poorly in a number skills assessment.[39] Parents with low skills are more likely to produce offspring who will leave the education system with poor qualifications. Poor education begets poor education. The failure of the education system to address low skills just stores up a bigger problem for future generations.

Costs to the Nation

Gove's education underclass seem destined to remain the school system's forgotten children. The post-Brexit Referendum Conservative Government unveiled the creation of new grammar schools as its flagship education policy.[40] Whatever the arguments over grammars, no one would claim they are the vehicle to address the country's basic skills problem. New measures to judge schools meanwhile prompted concerns that children with the poorest exam prospects will be excluded from schools to maximize their headline test scores.[41] And the National Audit Office warned that state schools faced the biggest real-terms cuts in a generation.[42]

Apart from the costs to individuals, the financial costs to the nation are substantial. The annual cost to the UK has been estimated to be around £20.2 billion, or about 1.3 per cent of the country's GDP – a similar figure to that produced for the consequences of low-income mobility as a whole.[43] This is likely to be an underestimate since the study considered only the impact of lower earnings and unemployment on individuals. Poor skills lead to poor health and higher criminality as well.

The most damaging penalty for failing to provide the education basics for 10 million people are the societal divisions this creates. The riots of 2011 were an explosion of the anger and resentment normally simmering just beneath the veneer of an ordered British society.[44] Recent political voting patterns suggest a stronger disenfranchisement picking up steam.

CHAPTER 6

Britain's Privately Educated Elites

The Country's Most Famous School

Amongst the idyllic English landscapes by Turner and Constable and the instantly recognizable masterpieces of Michelangelo and van Gogh hangs its portrait in the National Gallery in London. Only one work on permanent display in one of the world's finest collections of European art depicts an educational institution.

A beautiful white chapel stands as it does today amid the school's distinctive buildings on the banks of the River Thames. Though he probably finished the artwork later on in Venice, art historians believe the Italian painter Canaletto produced his original sketch of the scene around 1747.[1] The painting is a vivid reminder of how long the world's most famous school has commanded a prominent role in our national life. No, it is not Hogwarts. It is, of course, Eton College.

When Canaletto painted the school, Eton was already 300 years old and had produced a host of prime ministers, famous writers and scientists.[2] In 1440 King Henry VI had established Eton as a pure engine of social mobility: providing free education for seventy poor boys to go on to King's College, Cambridge. But then, as now, the need to finance the school meant it had no choice but to charge fees for the children whose families were able to afford it.

That model has had remarkable success over six centuries: Eton continues to influence modern public life in Britain in the early twenty-first century, nearly 600 years after it was founded. 'Probably the battle of Waterloo was won on the playing fields of Eton, but the opening battles of all subsequent wars have been lost there,' George Orwell claimed in his wartime essay, *The Lion and the Unicorn*, in 1941.[3] Orwell, who had enjoyed his time at Eton, used the famous words attributed to the Duke of Wellington to argue that an outdated British class system was hampering the war effort. But eighty years on, Eton, alongside the nation's other leading independent schools, is winning the battle that matters most. Far from decaying, the ruling class is in rude health.

A 2012 study of the school and university backgrounds of 8,000 of the country's most prominent people across a range of professions found Eton produced 330 leading people – 4 per cent of the nation's elites – including the Prime Minister, the Archbishop of Canterbury, and many more illustrious names.[4] It is an impressive number for one school; particularly given there are over 4,000 secondary schools across the country, both state and privately funded.

David Cameron was the nineteenth prime minister educated at Eton. And the inner circle of fellow Etonians who surrounded Cameron prompted one of his closest allies, Michael Gove, to criticize the clique of education elites at the heart of Government.[5] Apart from everything else, Etonians are adept at deflecting and assimilating any opposition. 'What chance have you got against a tie and a crest?' the singer-songwriter Paul Weller wrote in a 1982 song entitled

'Eton Rifles'. Weller's lyrics were an angry protest against Eton and the enduring elites presiding over the country. In 2009, much to Weller's chagrin, Cameron declared it was one of his favourite records when he was a young man at Eton, apparently not picking up on the feelings of injustice the song expressed.[6]

It is not just in Government but in all walks of public and professional life that Etonians flourish. In 2015 London's Mayor, Boris Johnson, himself Eton-educated, used the race for an Oscar between two privately educated actors to highlight the lack of state-educated actors Britain produces.[7] The Eton-educated actor Eddie Redmayne edged out his Harrovian rival Benedict Cumberbatch to win the 2015 best actor award. Johnson argued it was 'decades since we had a culture of bright kids from poor backgrounds who exuberantly burst down the doors of the establishment'.

Alumni of the Clarendon schools, made up of Eton and Harrow and seven other prestigious public schools, are 94 times more likely to be members of the British elite than those who attended any other school, another study found.[8] Even this figure may underestimate the 'propulsive power' of the schools. It is based on how likely former students are to feature in *Who's Who* – a catalogue of British professional elites. The country's public school boys made up a larger share of leaders 120 years ago, yet this may be because modern elites shy away from public attention. Public school old boys once sought fame serving the nation overseas as military or political leaders; now they are just as likely to hide away in offshore tax havens as hedge-fund managers.

Private Elites

In a 2012 study the Sutton Trust found that ten exclusive private schools supplied one in eight of Britain's elites. The ten schools were: Eton, Winchester, Charterhouse, Rugby, Westminster, Marlborough, Dulwich, Harrow, St Paul's Boys' School and Wellington College. Just under half of top people in Britain – 45 per cent – had attended a private school, although these make up only 7 per cent of all the country's schools.

Figure 6.1 shows the proportion of privately educated leaders across a range of different professions. The data reveal unlikely education bedfellows. Leading people in law and the armed services are among the most likely to have been privately educated; prominent figures in popular music and the police force on the other hand are the least likely, but still well above 7 per cent of those at the top.

A glittering array of private school alumni range from some of the country's most loved actors such as Jeremy Irons, Daniel Day-Lewis, Hugh Laurie, Rowan Atkinson and Kate Winslet to prominent broadcasters including Jeremy Paxman, Tony Blackburn, Jeremy Clarkson and the Dimbleby brothers. Famous sportsmen included Chris Hoy, Alastair Cook, Jonny Wilkinson and Tim Henman; leading musical talents, meanwhile, included Brian Eno, Lily Allen and Charlotte Church.

Another Sutton Trust study in 2016 found three-quarters (74 per cent) of the top judiciary (in the High Court and

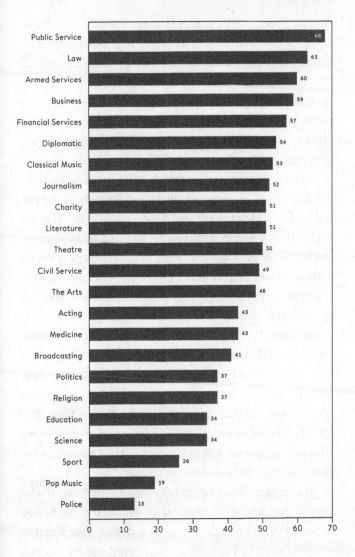

Figure 6.1
Percentage in selected professions who were privately educated (2012).[9]

Appeals Court), 71 per cent of the top military brass (two-star generals and above) and over half of leading print journalists, bankers and medics were privately educated.[10] Several studies have replicated these findings. The privately educated not only make up large proportions of today's political and professional elites, but leading people in other areas of public life, including the film and TV industry, the arts, music and sport.

'In every single sphere of British influence, the upper echelons of power in 2013 are held overwhelmingly by the privately educated or the affluent middle class. To me from my background, I find that truly shocking,' said Sir John Major, the former state-educated prime minister. 'Our education system should help children out of the circumstances in which they were born, not lock them into the circumstances in which they were born.'[11]

Reprising Wellington's famous words, the government-funded Social Mobility Commission found Britain's elites had been 'formed on the playing fields of independent schools'. In 2014 it reported that 50 per cent of members of the House of Lords, 44 per cent of the *Sunday Times* Rich List, 43 per cent of newspaper columnists, 35 per cent of the national rugby team and 33 per cent of the England cricket team had attended independent schools.[12]

In 2012 over one-third (36 per cent) of British medal winners in the London Olympics were educated at fee-paying schools.[13] The findings prompted a debate over whether Olympic sport had become elitist, missing out on sporting talent across the country. At least a third of the '100 British celebrities who really matter' – a list compiled for the *Daily*

Mail in 2010 – had also attended fee-paying schools. They included Simon Cowell, Sienna Miller, Holly Willoughby, Jude Law, Eddie Izzard, Catherine Zeta-Jones, Chris Martin (of the band Coldplay), Richard Branson and the footballer Frank Lampard.[14]

Higher Echelons

Another recurring finding is that the higher you climb up the career ladder in modern Britain, the more likely you are to be privately educated. While a third of MPs attended independent schools, half of the Cabinet in 2015 did so. Half of leading lawyers were privately educated compared with 70 per cent of High Court judges. Half of leading bankers went to private schools; yet over 70 per cent of those working in exclusive hedge funds and private equity firms did so.[15]

This pattern for the highest achievers is observed for film actors too, with over two-thirds (67 per cent) of British winners of Oscars having been educated at independent schools.[16] One of the few industries to buck the trend is popular music, where just over four-fifths (81 per cent) of British solo BRIT winners were state-educated. Although in classical music the pattern is reversed: three-quarters (75 per cent) of British Classic BRIT winners attended private schools.

Staying Power

The data for recent decades suggests these proportions of privately educated elites have stayed remarkably constant in many professions. In law, for example, 76 per cent of top judges had attended private schools in the late 1980s, 75 per cent by the mid-2000s and 74 per cent in 2016.[17]

The same can be said for leading news journalists, despite the profound changes experienced by the media industry in the early twenty-first century. Just over half (51 per cent) of editors, presenters and prominent commentators in 2016 were privately educated. This is slightly lower than the 54 per cent of leading news journalists educated in private schools in 2006, but higher than the 49 per cent of top journalists in 1986.[18]

Research by *The Times* found little change in the percentage of privately educated people selected for honours over the past sixty years: nearly half of the recipients of knighthoods and above in 2015 were privately educated. The figure – 46 per cent – had hardly changed since 1955, when it was 50 per cent.[19]

Looking at the last twenty-five years of Oscars, meanwhile, the proportion of privately educated British winners has remained remarkably stable at 60 per cent, with over a quarter (27 per cent) from state grammar schools and the remainder (13 per cent) from state comprehensives. This is despite the changing make-up of the state sector, including the phasing out of grammar schools during the period in which these actors were educated.

Business leaders buck this trend. But this is because far more foreigners now run businesses in Britain. The proportion of FTSE 100 chief executives educated at independent schools has fallen from 70 per cent in the late 1980s, to 54 per cent in the late 2000s, to 34 per cent in 2016.

The proportion of privately educated Members of Parliament fell from 49 per cent in 1979 and 51 per cent in 1983 to around a third in more recent Parliaments.[20] In 2015 the proportion was 32 per cent.[21] But the education backgrounds of MPs holding the most senior Government positions in Cabinet have stayed fairly constant. Half of the Conservative Cabinet in 2015 was privately educated; this was lower than the preceding 2010 Coalition Cabinet (62 per cent), but slightly higher than Tony Blair's Cabinet (44 per cent) immediately after the 2005 general election. The 2016 Conservative Cabinet appointed by Prime Minister Theresa May had only 30 per cent privately educated members – the lowest proportion since the Labour Prime Minister Clement Attlee in 1945.[22]

Comparable data for previous decades is harder to come by, but sociologists made similar observations when studying elites in the early 1970s. They found 'the extraordinary near monopoly exerted by the public schools in general, the influence of the Clarendon schools in particular, and of Eton especially, over elite recruitment in this country.'[23]

Future Runes

The emerging evidence on the latest generations trying to climb the first rungs of the career ladder indicates these patterns are likely to continue for future leaders. Senior newspaper editors reported that private school alumni exhibited the stronger skills and attributes needed to progress in a highly competitive industry at an earlier age. They reported that the most recent recruits to the national news media are more likely to come from privileged backgrounds than those from previous generations.[24]

These arguments echo those articulated by a number of prominent actors that the acting industry is increasingly becoming the preserve of those from more privileged backgrounds.[25] The data shows those from working-class backgrounds made up 18 per cent of people in the cultural and creative industries compared with just under 35 per cent in the general population. Publishing was among the industries with a particularly middle-class make-up. 'These findings clearly puncture romantic notions of these industries as paragons of merit and accessibility,' the authors concluded. Access to an agent, entering drama school and taking on unpaid work were the reasons cited for the increasing lack of diversity.[26]

Over a third of recent entrants in the financial services industry were found to have attended private schools.[27] A report on the socio-economic diversity in the civil service Fast Stream found it had a less diverse intake than the student population at the University of Oxford.[28]

Academic Benefits

This career success is underpinned by the significant academic and social benefits a private education offers. An analysis in 1984 reported that private schools produced a remarkable improvement in academic performance between 1961 and 1981. By the end of this period 45 per cent of students were achieving three or more A levels, compared with 14.5 per cent at the beginning. This compared with an increase in the state sector from 3.1 per cent to 7.1 per cent.[29]

In 2016 just under half of A-level entries (48.7 per cent)

from pupils based in the 495 private schools represented by the Independent Schools Council were awarded an A* or A grade, compared with just over a quarter (25.8 per cent) of entries that had done so nationally.[30]

One of the problems with these types of comparisons is they don't take into account that many highly selective independent schools attract high-achieving students to begin with; it is unclear how much the final A-level results are due to what the school is adding, and how much they are due to outside factors associated with the students themselves.

Private school pupils are on average two years ahead academically of their counterparts in state schools by the age of 16, even taking into account the social background and prior attainment of children.[31] This equates to independently educated pupils gaining an extra 0.64 of a grade for each of their GCSE examinations at age 16.

Private schools boast an impressive record in the numbers of pupils they send to the country's most prestigious universities, who supply the lion's share of graduates for many elite careers. This is demonstrated at its most extreme in admissions to Oxford and Cambridge. A Sutton Trust study found four private schools and one sixth-form college sent more pupils to Oxbridge over three years than 2,000 other schools and colleges across the UK.[32] The five were made up of four private schools – Westminster, Eton, St Paul's, St Paul's Girls' School – and the state-funded Hills Road sixth-form college.

Meanwhile 100 schools, making up 3 per cent of schools with sixth forms and sixth-form colleges in the UK, accounted for just under a third (just under 32 per cent) of admissions to Oxbridge during the three years. These schools were composed of 84 independent schools and 16 grammar schools. A separate analysis found private-school students were 55 times more likely to win a place at Oxbridge than students at state schools who qualified for free school meals.[33]

The superior academic results of privately educated pupils explain much of these university enrolment figures; studies suggest they are also more likely to apply to prestigious degree courses, an indication of the extra advice and support they receive. Pupils from top-performing independent schools on average made twice as many applications to leading universities than their peers from state comprehensive schools with similar average A- level results.[34]

But once at university, a more mixed picture emerges. Privately schooled students are less likely to leave university with a first- or an upper-second-class degree than state-educated graduates.[35] The study reported 73 per cent of independent school students graduated from English universities in 2013–14 with the two top degree grades. This compared with 82 per cent of state school leavers.

This gap remained when taking into account the subject studied at university. But the difference disappeared for students from different school backgrounds with the highest A-level grades. One explanation for the differences is that private schools maximize the academic potential of their pupils, but many state school pupils achieve lower A-level grades than they might otherwise have done if given more support.

Despite this, other studies have found an increasing pay

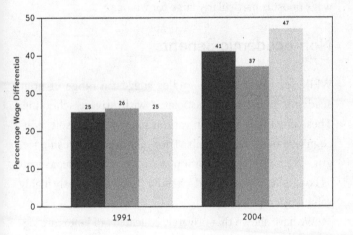

Figure 6.2
Private / State school wage differentials for 33–34-year-olds.[36]

■ All
■ Men
■ Women

premium from studying at private school.[37] Our own analysis of the figures confirms these wage differentials, presented in Figure 6.2. In 1991, privately educated 33–34-year-olds were earning on average 25 per cent more than their otherwise similar state-educated counterparts. In 2004, the pay premium for privately educated 33–34-year-olds had increased to 41 per cent more than their state-educated peers. This wage boost is particularly large for women.

Non-academic Benefits

While less quantifiable, studies suggest a range of non-academic benefits are associated with private schooling. These attributes are given various names: social, soft, non-cognitive or essential skills. They include drive, resilience, grit, effective communication, a strong work ethic, as well as confidence, 'polish' and 'character' – all apparently highly valued by employers.

We have shown that privately educated graduates are significantly more likely to enter top occupations. But research also shows they manage to do this with the same academic grades as their state-school peers. A study found a 'sizeable difference' in entry rates into elite professions by the type of school attended.[38] This could be due to unmeasured personal assets and advantages, including human capital (wider knowledge, skills and attributes); cultural capital (for example, being able to converse on a range of topics during interviews); and financial capital (money allowing the privately educated graduate to survive on unpaid internships and low salaries during the early years of their career).

These attributes, whether social, cultural or financial, may partly account for another finding: the higher chances of privately educated applicants gaining places at elite universities. The proportion of university entrants going to Oxbridge from the 30 top-performing independent schools was nearly twice that of those from the 30 top-performing grammar schools – despite having similar average A-level scores.[39]

Other research has suggested these social skills are what elite firms demand when defining the 'talent' they are seeking from potential recruits.[40] Powerful alumni networks meanwhile maintain strong links among former students in many private schools, yielding invaluable connections that open up work opportunities. They are conspicuous by their absence in the state sector.[41] Even at Cambridge and Oxford, public school products can stick together in their own cliques, embodied most famously by the Bullingdon Club at Oxford.[42]

No place nurtures these life skills more than Eton, and its alumni are feted for having a particular charm and confidence, enabling them to prosper in life after school.[43] Indeed it is the pastoral care offered that is the reason given for the escalating fees at Eton and other leading private schools – raising concerns the schools are out of bounds for all but the most privileged.[44]

The Significance of Rising Fees

Focusing on private schools provides a partial picture of the educational backgrounds of Britain's elites. Another striking feature is how few state-comprehensive educated leaders remain once the numbers of private and grammar school alumni are combined.[45] Studies also show the country's leading state schools are highly socially exclusive.[46] But private schools are of particular interest from a social mobility perspective precisely because they have been so successful in producing high achievers over successive generations. The problem is that they are only accessible to the small minority of the population able to afford the fees required to get in.

In 2015 a survey found parents were paying more than £15,500 a year on average to send their son or daughter to a fee-paying school.[47] At Eton the annual fees were just under £36,000 a year.[48] These charges are prohibitive for most people; the estimate for the median household disposable income for the same year was £25,600.[49]

Private schools are increasingly out of reach for all but the most wealthy. One analysis suggested fees had quadrupled between 1990 and 2015, putting the average price of sending two children to private school above half a million pounds – around double the average house price in the UK.[50] Even with two parents working, many middle-class families would struggle to educate their children privately. Another analysis suggested fees were at their least affordable for middle-class parents since at least the 1960s.[51]

At boarding schools, including Eton, the proportion of places taken by children from wealthy families abroad is steadily increasing.[52] Another study found independent schools award on average just under 8 per cent of their income to bursaries and scholarships; this proportion was lower for the highest performing schools. Only half of this money to offset fees was going on means-tested bursaries for poorer families.[53]

Social Mobility Concerns

The combination of educational success and lack of access for children from all but the wealthiest backgrounds makes private schools powerful vehicles of intergenerational persistence. They are the glue maintaining the stickiness at the top of British society. And the glue appears to be getting stronger.

But their success poses major challenges for the nation as a whole. The risk of having such high proportions of people at the top of society from the wealthiest homes is they have a limited perspective or even a 'group think' mentality when deciding on issues that impact on the 93 per cent of the population from less affluent backgrounds.[54] This could have societal as well as economic costs. In his 1958 book, *The Rise of the Meritocracy*, Michael Young warned of the dire consequences of a society where most of the population have scant chance of climbing the social ladder.[55] We will come back to Young's prophetic warnings.

The country is also failing to fully nurture talent from the majority of the population unable to afford private school fees. As a country we are missing out on our biggest talent pool, fishing in the same small pond for generation after generation.

On current evidence, the private school elites will continue to prosper in Britain for the foreseeable future. There is little appetite for tackling the educational inequalities they create. Eton meanwhile is predicted to maintain its special role as 'the chief nurse of England's statesmen' for centuries to come.[56] It is also likely to retain its unique place among the national treasures on display at the National Gallery. As in so many other areas, the privately educated make up much of the arts establishment: one last astonishing fact is that every director of the National Gallery since it was established in 1855 has been educated at an independent school.

PART THREE

Improving Social Mobility

The Way Ahead

The Way Ahead

Society is not short on advocates claiming to have the solution to Britain's low social mobility. The amount of evidence underpinning their claims can be inversely proportional to how passionately the views are held. Dig beneath the surface and the arguments crumble away.

The evidence suggests there is no one panacea that will magically enhance social mobility. Life just is not that simple. Reducing inequality, enhancing economic growth and equalizing education are all necessary in the fight to open up opportunities to people from less advantaged backgrounds. But none are sufficient on their own to win the battle. Enhancing social mobility – both at the top and bottom – is likely to involve working on several interconnecting fronts. Navigating a way ahead requires careful balance rather than extreme measures.

Reducing Extreme Inequality

The growing divide in life's resources has taken its toll on many Britons. We are a society of unequals: not just in terms of the money we earn, but the wealth we own, the attitudes we have, and the political beliefs we hold. We might as well admit we have fragmented into different tribes. Britain has become a country split economically, geographically and politically.

So why not just close society's divide: stop worrying about climbing the rungs of the income ladder, just narrow the gaps between them? If we narrowed the earnings differential between cleaners and chief executives we would replicate the high mobility witnessed in Scandinavian countries, so the argument goes. Our social elites would be less fearful of falling down life's ladder. There would be less to lose.

The counter argument is that income inequality is good for society and the economy: it sharpens incentives and offers just rewards for those who want to improve their lives through their own talent and hard work. Introducing his memorable 'cornflakes box' model of social mobility, Boris Johnson argued it would be wrong to try to stamp out inequality: it is an invaluable spur to economic activity and wealth creation. The wealth gap, according to Johnson, should be tolerated as long as there are healthy levels of social (or cornflake) mobility: 'There are too many cornflakes who aren't being given a good enough chance to rustle and hustle their way to the top. We gave the packet a good shake in the 1960s; and Mrs Thatcher gave it another good shake in the 1980s.'[1]

Johnson's defence of unbridled capitalism highlights the problem with the equality argument: for every advocate there is an equally ardent (and vocal) opponent. The debate about whether to pursue equality of outcomes or equality of opportunities has polarized political opinion for hundreds of years. It can split ministerial siblings. In 2017 Universities

Minister Jo Johnson (Boris's brother) took the unprecedented step of attacking university chiefs for lining their pockets with unjustifiably high salaries.[2] For one Johnson at least, inequality has its limits.

Raising tax rates for the rich may be a gamble in today's global economy: if the wealthy leave Britain's shores to pay less tax elsewhere, that will mean less, not more, revenue for the national purse. Yet Stanford University Professor Cristobal Young concludes that far from fleeing higher taxes, financial elites are surprisingly reluctant to leave home. Young found that 84 per cent of the world's wealthiest individuals, as listed in *Forbes* magazine, still live in the country of their birth. Most billionaires live where they were born or where their careers first blossomed. Only 5 per cent moved abroad after making their fortunes. Famous billionaires such as Richard Branson who relocate to tropical tax havens are the exception not the rule.

'The British elite live in Britain, the Chinese elite live in China, and the American elite live in America,' says Young. Global financial elites are more likely to die than to move to a different country. Analysing 45 million US tax returns, Young found that America's millionaires are half as likely as the poorest residents to move away from their home state. Family and social roots become more important than financial savings for the wealthy. The rich act as 'embedded elites' rather than 'transitory millionaires'.[3]

Yet that still leaves a nagging question for fans of redistributing taxes to the poor: it is how families deploy their resources that is key to whether they promote the advancement of their children. This tension is at the heart of the social welfare debate: safety nets for the most vulnerable can become disincentives to progress in life and stymie upward mobility. Some argue it is the unintended incentives to stay out of work and on welfare benefits that have created an immobile underclass increasingly disconnected from the rest of the population.[4] In life it is not what you spend that counts, but how you spend it.

The *Great Gatsby* Curve highlights the link between inequality and social mobility for a range of countries. This is a two-way relationship, but the direction of causation very plausibly flows from more inequality to less mobility. Extreme inequality of incomes when children are younger leads to greater inequality of opportunity. And elites made up of the privileged few are less inclined to support redistributive policies giving those lower down society's ranks a greater chance of moving up and displacing them at the top.

The transformation of American children under the age of thirteen who move to districts with less inequality echoes the global evidence pointing to a causal link between inequality in early life and later opportunity.[5] When Raj Chetty analysed data from the Moving to Opportunity experiment in the US he found higher social mobility levels for younger children who moved to more equal places. Movers were more likely to attend college and command higher earnings in later life compared to children left behind. Longer exposure to equality led to better outcomes.

This is supported by the research literature on child development during the early years.[6] Children are deprived not just because of the lack of material basics money can buy – food, a place to sleep – but the absence of a stable, consistent and nurturing environment in the home with adult role models holding decent jobs in the local community. Pre-schools gaps in development are large. US researchers found a 30 million word gap by the age of four: a child from a professional family will hear 45 million words, a working-class child 26 million, and a child on welfare only 13 million.[7] It is hard for Britain's detached elite to comprehend what it means to grow up on the other side of the tracks.

Inequality's crushing hand now reaches well beyond the formative years into early adulthood, when latent talent can still be spotted. The conditions experienced by workers have a profound impact on the opportunities they have to progress up the career ladder. A generation ago even lowly cleaners employed by multinationals had a chance to train and rise up the ranks if they worked hard enough.[8] Now, employed on short-term contracts, with few rights, by outside service providers, they are stuck beneath an opportunity ceiling. Furthermore, part-time study is in rapid decline among mature students.[9] Inequality impedes the prospects of social mobility's second-chancers.

The critical debate over inequality is whether current levels of it impair or encourage social mobility, in both absolute and relative terms. And the evidence suggests we have reached a tipping point: those on the lower rungs of the ladder are peering up at such an impossibly steep climb that they would rather step off than step up.

International comparisons reveal that when inequality in a country is too high, families from lower income backgrounds invest less in education and skills, or 'human capital'.[10] They lag further behind richer families in basic numeracy and literacy skills. It's little surprise that this hinders national economic growth, since the talents of a large swathe of the population are being squandered.

What distinguishes Britain (and the United States) from other countries are the excessively high earnings commanded by university graduates compared with other school leavers. The graduate premium in Britain – where graduates on average earn nearly 60 per cent more than non-graduates – is double that in Canada or Australia. 'A labour market in which college graduates earn so much more than others is not only resulting in greater inequality, it is also sending a signal to the rich that their extra resources should be invested strongly in the education of the next generation,' argues the Canadian economist Miles Corak. 'Making the tax system more progressive hits two targets with one arrow, it not only reduces inequality in the here and now but in levelling outcomes in the current generation it also diminishes disparities in the next.'[11]

The evidence suggests that it is time for the Government to act: by raising inheritance tax, for example, and closing the tax loopholes allowing the super-wealthy to entrench their privilege. It cannot be fair that a teacher on £30,000 a year will pay a higher percentage of their income in tax than a billionaire gaining £300 million a year from global investments. And, as many wealthy philanthropists have concluded, access to unearned wealth undermines the incentive for their children to work. Higher inheritance tax would force many families to sell their expensive properties allowing others to get on the property ladder, off-limits to all but the wealthy in places such as London. The extra revenues generated could be used to pay key public sector workers more.

A pragmatic way forward is to limit excessive income and wealth inequality and aspire to improve social mobility. This argument is increasingly being made by social scientists in the face of falling absolute mobility, although it is by no means a new one. A long time ago, writing in the 1930s, the historian R. H. Tawney argued in his book *Equality* that promoting opportunity depends 'not only upon an open road, but upon an equal start'.[12] We need to lift cornflakes stuck at the bottom, and shake the box differently. Agreeing on the limits to damaging levels of inequality might just be possible. That means enhancing lower salaries and ending many of the tax loopholes enjoyed by the rich, including off-shore tax havens. It could foster more inclusive economic growth and perhaps solve Britain's productivity puzzle.

Growing the Economy for All

Which brings us to another apparent panacea: growing ourselves out of trouble. If we boost economic growth we do not need to worry about inequality, or so the argument goes. Everyone would enjoy an increasing share of the cake, as the economic cake gets bigger overall. We would replicate the golden era of booming absolute mobility in the post-war years.

Some believe that social mobility is primarily driven by the availability of good jobs created by an expanding economy.[13] This is the 'room at the top' argument: the claim is that it is the demand from the world of work that matters, not the supply of educational talent to fill it.

Most politicians prefer to focus on improving absolute mobility. What could be more popular than a world in which all travellers in life's caravan are advancing more quickly than their forebears? When he was prime minister, Gordon Brown likened this to a 'national crusade'.[14] The plan rested on the (not so) small matter of rejuvenating Britain's ailing economy.

The flaw with this plan is that, more recently, economic growth has mostly benefitted the better-off.[15] The evidence shows that, unlike for long periods in the past when productivity and median wages grew at broadly similar rates, in the recent past median wage growth has lagged behind productivity growth.[16] Therefore, 'faster growth is necessary but not sufficient to restore higher intergenerational income mobility,' conclude Lawrence Katz and Alan Krueger in their deconstruction of declining absolute mobility in the United States. 'Evidence suggests that, to increase income mobility, policy-makers should focus on raising middle-class and lower-income household incomes.'[17]

Nine in ten American children born in 1940 went on to earn a higher income than their parents; but only one in two Americans born in the 1980s did so. The economists estimate that three-quarters of this decline in absolute mobility levels is down to widening income inequality, and a quarter is down to weaker economic growth. All the indicators point to a similarly bleak picture in Britain.

America and Britain's emerging industrial model in the global economy of the twenty-first century is that companies directly employ elite university graduates as core workers, and contract out lower-level work to temping agencies and other contractors. For the global executives and private equity owners, that's the obvious way to maximize profits: invest in talent and contract out basic work. But it has created a two-tier system between those pursuing the 'royal route' of seamless career progression and those stuck in dead-end, insecure jobs without a future. 'It used to be that General Motors had people throughout the education and income distributions working there,' says Katz. 'Whereas, today's large firms, the Apples and Goldmans, tend to mainly directly employ college graduates and elites.'[18]

In the post-war years society's stragglers at the rear of the caravan could at least comfort themselves that life had got better compared with previous generations. Improving their relative position did not matter as much. Young adults of the twenty-first century are the generation whose luck ran out. Not only are they less likely to leapfrog ahead of others, they are moving more slowly than their forebears. Rising tides and trickle-down effects are meaningless promises from another millennium.

Amid global economic gloom, we need more than ever to nurture all our talents and pursue a targeted uplift for the lowest earners. Improving social mobility may offer one route to begin to solve the country's productivity puzzle.

Realistic Aspirations for Education

The romantic notion of education as the great social leveller is implanted in our national consciousness in fact and fiction. The country's first female prime minister, Margaret Thatcher, was the daughter of a shopkeeper who went on to study at the local grammar school and Oxford University.[19] Adele, the singer-songwriter from Tottenham in North London who has sold 100 million records worldwide, attributes her success to gaining a place at the BRIT school for performing arts.[20] Sir Harry Kroto, who won a Nobel prize for chemistry, was the son of immigrants who secured a scholarship to attend Bolton Grammar School.[21]

Education's power to catapult a lucky few into a different social class is a recurring theme in British literature. *The History Boys* is a popular play recounting the halcyon days when grammar school students from working-class backgrounds competed with private schools to win a place at the country's most prestigious universities.[22] Set in Cutlers' Grammar School, Sheffield, a fictional boys' school, the play pokes fun at the headmaster's lofty academic aspirations. But it is also a reflection on competing views of what education is for – learning for learning's sake or maximizing students' test scores. The author, Alan Bennett, was himself a product of the grammar school system, and won a scholarship to Oxford.

Our education system does a miraculous job of counterbalancing the income, wealth and cultural disparities in wider society. It can transform individual lives. The numbers of children on free school meals passing national school benchmarks at age 16 and going on to university has rocketed over recent decades. It is just that the middle classes have leaped further ahead.

Academy schools set up by the Blair government as part of a remedial school improvement programme raised pupil attainment, despite serving disadvantaged communities.[23]

Some London academies with students from a range of backgrounds – Mossbourne, King Solomon's – remain top-performing schools. The same is true of some charter schools (free from local school district control) in urban areas in the United States.[24]

The age-old challenge is replicating these transformational examples across the nation as a whole. The history of education is littered with singular success stories that last for a limited time, or fail to be fulfilled for more than a few schools. The truth is schools can only do so much. They are governed by the '80:20 rule': on average 80 per cent of the variation in children's school results is due to individual and family characteristics, while the remaining 20 per cent is due to what happens in school.[25] Some schools excel by producing better results with very similar intakes of children. But the idea that teachers on their own can cancel out extreme inequalities outside the school gates is fanciful.

Randomized trials investigating interventions in England's schools have found positive but relatively small gains in children's core attainment.[26] Britain's evidence-led education movement shows how hard it is to raise school results, particularly for pupils from disadvantaged backgrounds, and points to a much thornier problem: getting more schools to adopt the teaching practices that have already been shown to work well.

The studies confirm what all good teachers know: what matters most is the quality of interaction between teachers and children in the classroom. Structural changes in schools – reducing class sizes by small amounts, for example, or developing new types of schools – have little or no impact on the children's progress. Intensive work by teachers, engaging with children in small groups, or offering one-to-one tutoring make the largest immediate impact on the attainment of pupils. Catch-up classes for children who have fallen behind their peers tend not to reduce the learning gaps. There's no substitute for getting it right with schoolchildren first time around.

Most interventions investigated by the Education Endowment Foundation (EEF) are no better than 'teaching as usual' in other schools: only around a quarter of EEF studies show enough impact to warrant larger scale-up trials involving more schools. The most promising programmes boost students' progress by an extra three months in a school year; yet the effect shrinks when scaled up to hundreds of schools. Scaling up is hard to do. Surveys of teachers reveal greater recognition of educational evidence, but little sign of more focus on the classroom approaches shown by research to be most effective.[27]

We put unrealistic expectations on education by itself to be the great social leveller. That is the message from Baltimore to San Jose to London: it is the mix of less divided, less segregated and more aspirant, stable and connected communities in the vicinity of good schools that matters. A good education system is a necessary but not sufficient condition to improve social mobility.

International evidence demonstrates that education proves its worth in a more equal environment. The creation of comprehensive schools in egalitarian Finland during the 1970s reduced the country's intergenerational income persistence by several percentage points.[28] Equitable education in a society without extreme inequality aids social mobility.

Yet we cannot help seeking the educational miracle cure that will wipe out attainment gaps between the rich and poor and solve poverty as well as society's other ills dumped at the school gates. The quest for the 'London effect' is a case in point.[29] Researchers rushed to uncover the formula that had transformed London's schools into the country's stand-out performers. The success was put down first to the 'London Challenge' secondary school reforms.[30] But since this combined several programmes, it was hard to evaluate.[31] And similar programmes in the Black Country and Greater Manchester had failed to produce the same results. Another study meanwhile suggested London's turnaround was more likely due to improving primary schools.[32]

But as with so many quests, the rush to find answers had lost sight of the real story. Economist Simon Burgess delivered a humbling message: the London effect could be explained away when the diverse composition of pupils was taken into account.[33] Burgess argued the headlong rush to find the magic bullets behind the London effect was overlooking the real achievement: the dynamism of London's increasingly diverse population, composed of children whose parents had come from all over the world. 'Sustaining a large, successful and reasonably integrated multi-ethnic school system containing pupils from every country in the world and speaking more than 300 languages is a great thing. To my mind, this is what we should be celebrating about the London education system.'[34]

The social composition of London's population had indeed changed. London's central areas – those involved in the London Challenge – underwent a dramatic gentrification. We have documented this by tracking the percentage of dual-university-graduate families and average family incomes over twenty years. As Figure 7.1 reveals, London is now the stand-out capital of graduate coupling.

By 2016 a third of London families had two parents with degrees. Average family incomes meanwhile in London and the South-East pulled away from those in other areas of the country.[35] Demographic change has in large part driven the capital's education turnaround, and indeed its improved performance relative to other regions on a wide range of economic and social outcomes, including wages, health and crime.[36]

We must, difficult as it is, do away with idealistic notions that education entirely on its own will solve all.

Unrepresentative Elites

Why should we make special efforts to enable more travellers from the rear of life's caravan to ascend to leading positions at the front? Because without change at the top first, other fundamental reforms are far less likely to occur. Improving relative social mobility unlocks parts of society that other policies are unable to reach.

Socially diverse elites make for better leaders and decision makers. They understand and empathize with the people they are meant to serve. They are less likely to suffer from the 'group think' and narrow perspectives that characterize homogenous ruling classes. 'It is entirely possible

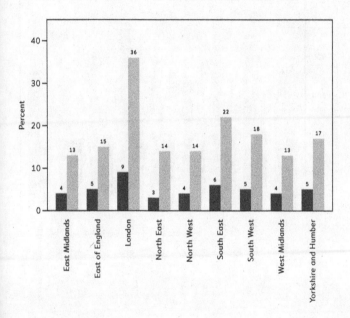

Figure 7.1
Percentage of dual-university-graduate families by region.

■ 1995
▨ 2016

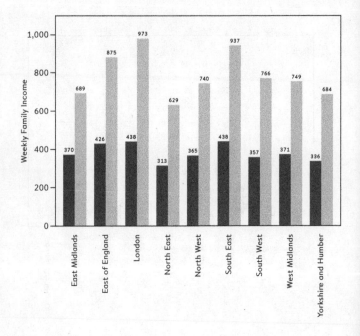

Figure 7.2
Average family income by region.[37]

■ 1994–5
■ 2015–6

for politicians to rely on advisors to advise, civil servants to devise policy solutions and journalists to report on their actions having all studied the same courses at the same universities, having read the same books, heard the same lectures and even being taught by the same tutors,' the Social Mobility Commission has argued. 'This risks narrowing the conduct of public life to a small few, who are very familiar with each other but far less familiar with the day-to-day challenges facing ordinary people in the country.'[38]

In *The Rise of the Meritocracy* the post-war social reformer Michael Young envisages a dystopian future for Britain dominated by a new 'meritocratic elite' that has exploited the education system to justify its position of power. Their trick would be to control what 'merit' constituted. They would justify their positions of power on the back of their superior academic results. 'The new class has the means at hand, and largely under its control, by which it reproduces itself,' Young argued. *The Rise of the Meritocracy* has been much misunderstood – much to Young's chagrin in later life.[39] Politicians now see meritocracy as a necessary condition for greater social mobility, not a sorting machine engineered by elites to retain their status. At the turn of the Millennium Tony Blair spoke of creating a new, meritocratic Britain 'where people should rise according to merit not birth.'[40] Fifteen years later, Theresa May became the latest prime minister to abuse the M-word. She too vowed to transform Britain into 'the great meritocracy of the world'.[41]

Young would doubtless have noted the irony that Britain's political masters now emerge from an exclusive academic route – epitomized by private schooling and Oxbridge degrees. Never have such a narrow academic few ruled over so many. Just one degree course – Philosophy, Politics and Economics (PPE) at Oxford – pervades British political life in a manner unmatched in any other democracy. According to one count, some 80 leading politicians and 40 prominent journalists were Oxford PPE graduates.[42]

There are concerns about the narrow focus of newsrooms made up of journalists all hailing from the same walks of the life.[43] The danger is that they see society from one shared vantage point, which influences their decisions about what news stories are covered. The veteran BBC journalist John Humphrys, from Welsh working-class stock, told researchers: 'You must reflect the population you serve, it seems to me. I just feel instinctively that if, say, 30/40/50/60 per cent of journalists at the BBC were public school it wouldn't be right.'

Indeed, the latest generations of children entering professions such as law or journalism are more likely to come from more prosperous homes, whilst less likely to score highly in cognitive tests at age 11 than previous cohorts.[44] According to this research, our elites are becoming posher and more privileged, but at the same time not so clever.

Others have bemoaned the odd rulings made by out-of-touch judges, who also hark from a tiny social elite.[45] Baroness Hale, the only woman judge in the Supreme Court at the time, warned that judges may lack common sense because they have lived sheltered lives. She said it was dangerous for the common law to rely upon the experience and common sense of a comparatively narrow section of society.[46] Exclusive 'magic circle' law firms and investment banks now seek talent from more diverse backgrounds to better reflect and understand the customers they work with. Improving social mobility has become core business rationale. 'Cognitive diversity', like gender or ethnic diversity, improves decision-making in the world of business.[47]

Greater social diversity among professional elites is beneficial in other ways. In medicine, general practitioners from less affluent backgrounds were more likely to work in practices serving the most deprived communities.[48] Research from the United States suggests that students from lower income groups may be more likely to pursue family medicine – a priority in many countries including Britain.[49] Studying in a more diverse medical school meanwhile may enable students to be better prepared to care for minority groups within society.

The actor Michael Sheen argues that the privileged makeup of the creative arts threatens the country's rich cultural diversity: the emergence of working-class writers and actors in the 1950s and 1960s (part of the post-war boom in social mobility) introduced different voices and perspectives in the theatre, in film and on television. Such alternative voices now may get lost altogether. 'That's what changed our country and our culture. If we only hear certain stories and certain voices we all lose out.'[50]

When wealthy elites dominate positions of power they are less likely to deliver policies that help to improve the lot of those from other backgrounds. The failure over successive generations to provide a well delivered and highly regarded alternative education for the hundreds of thousands of children leaving schools without any qualifications is partly because so few people in Government have the faintest idea about, or experience of, their needs. The education system has failed children with different talents – not necessarily the narrow analytical academic skills judged in school exams, but other attributes, be they creative, practical or vocational. Low mobility's legacy is a self-interested and self-perpetuating elite that is ineffectual for the rest of society.

Ruling elites drawn from a small slither of society are less interested in, and knowledgeable about, policy areas instrumental to influencing the prospects of people from other backgrounds. These policy areas can then fall victim to 'policy churn' – repeated Government reviews. These are not followed through, not informed by the failure of past initiatives, and are ignored by the media.[51]

This is especially true for the Cinderella sector of further education colleges, and indeed vocational education in general. On the announcement of yet another reform of vocational and technical routes for young people, Rachel Wolf, a former education adviser at 10 Downing Street, said: 'Journalists did not usually go to FE [further education] colleges, and neither do their children. Politicians – even Labour ones – are more and more likely to have gone through traditional, elite education routes; therefore their understanding and instinctive desire to protect FE is low.' According to Wolf, Government ministers and civil servants are unlikely to notice if things go wrong 'because the elite will not have friends who are experiencing disaster'.[52]

Immobility among the highest echelons is bad for future economic productivity. Nations led by narrow elites are less likely to make public investments that enhance economic activity. In sum, the leaders of life's caravan need to have trodden many different paths.

Rethinking Work and Education

IMPROVING ABSOLUTE MOBILITY

Being stuck has been a theme of this book: the same winners and losers at the top and bottom of society's ranks persisting from one generation to the next; the same entrenched debates failing to create a more mobile society. In the world of education and work, we remain stuck with a twentieth-century mind-set as we brace ourselves for a fast-changing twenty-first-century world.

We need a workplace that treats employees as a long-term investment essential for future economic growth rather than a resource to be exploited for quick profit. Training needs to be embraced not endured. And we need an education system that nurtures all talents, not one preoccupied with an academic race only the rich can win. Lifelong learning in a globalized knowledge economy will make the worlds of work and education indistinguishable. In short, we need a new model of work and education for improving social mobility.

Pay Progression and Productivity

Our social elites were more acceptable when there was something else to distract the rest of the population. The manufacturing industries of the nineteenth and twentieth centuries – founded on raw materials of coal, iron, steel and textiles – offered local occupations, job progression and decent pay. Unions ensured workers' rights. Those leaving school to work in factories, mines or docks enjoyed a clear career trajectory with stable employment. Many became respected pillars of society as foremen, supervisors or shop-floor managers.

The post-war boom of knowledge and service economy jobs – social mobility's golden age – was in retrospect only a temporary respite from a deeper industrial decline.[1] Many of Britain's former centres of economic vigour are now today's opportunity wastelands.[2] We are still mourning the loss of proud working communities destroyed when cheaper resources and labour became available overseas. We are still seeking a plan B.

Ruth Davison, leader of the Scottish Conservative Party, has asked how teenagers living in a pit town with no pit, a steel town with no steel or a factory town with no factory can see modern capitalism working for them. 'Is the route for social advancement a degree, student debt, moving to London to spend more than half their take-home pay on a room in a shared flat in Zone 6 and half of what's left commuting to their stagnant-wage job every day; knowing there is precisely zero chance of saving enough to ever own their own front door? Or is it staying put in a community that feels like it is being hollowed out from the inside?'[3]

Davison pinpoints the twin challenges of social mobility: enabling talent irrespective of background to get to the top of society (however defined), while encouraging people to live fulfilling lives in their local communities. In Britain there are programmes that catapult a lucky few into elite universities and prestigious professions.[4] But there is scant evidence of effective regional rejuvenation for those left behind. Our young are caught between a rock and a hard place. We need a new model of social mobility – one that seeks to improve both absolute and relative levels.[5]

This is a chance to re-establish the ladders of opportunity extending from the education system into the workplace that offer an alternative route to social mobility, recognizing merit in its many forms, creative, practical, technical as well as academic and social. The challenge is equalizing the other side of the social mobility equation: that relating to people's prospects during their entire lifetimes, long after traditional education is over.

Prospects for young unskilled Britons are bleak. The proliferation of short-term and temporary contracts in the economy harks back to the poor work conditions suffered in Victorian times.[6] Frozen wages signal an era of shrinking opportunity. And the rise of robots threatens to wipe out many middle-tier jobs, once the stepping stones for rewarding careers. The danger is that the future labour market will deepen the skills divide: offering limitless opportunities for the high-skilled and dead-end jobs for the low-skilled.

Yet this fast-changing workplace offers opportunities for Britain to boost productivity and absolute mobility levels. Intelligent machines will perform many tasks more reliably and efficiently than humans. But the skills that make us human – creativity, complex communication, multi-disciplinary thinking, innovation, emotional intelligence – will be increasingly valued.[7] Britain's globally successful music and entertainment industries may offer lessons for other business sectors.[8]

Automation's advance is likely to increase the importance of apprenticeships. The interpersonal and technical skills that machines cannot master will be learned on the job. The status of the 'learn while you earn' route has been lost despite evidence that some degree-level apprenticeships can produce higher earnings than many 'academic' degrees. A key challenge is how to change the hearts and minds of British employers so that they embrace the Germanic culture of valuing quality training in the workplace.

Britain is losing the race for skilled workers in the global economy. England has more people than other comparable countries in elementary jobs requiring few skills. Just under one-third of workers reported that their job required less than secondary school education to perform – more than in many other countries. The OECD found the low-skilled were more likely than better-skilled workers to hold a fixed-term or temporary contract, or work without a contract.

The OECD urged the country to make 'better use of paths combining education and training in workplaces'. In England only one in ten young adults with low skills work while studying – half the proportion earning and learning in Australia and Canada. The contrast with the more mobile Anglophone countries is once again telling.

Combining education with workplace learning smooths the transition to the labour market, helping young people to develop basic skills and providing 'meaningful learning alternatives to students who are more practically oriented'. In

Germany and Austria the majority of low-skilled adults who report working while studying are apprentices.[9]

There are signs the tide may be turning in Britain. Prestigious universities and organizations, including the BBC, now offer high-level apprenticeships as an alternative to degree study.[10] Parity of esteem is essential. Apprentices require respected portable qualifications akin to university degrees that stand the test of the time. The Scandinavian and Germanic countries also show how effective retraining systems can be for people when they lose their jobs.[11] Re-employed people return into jobs that are as good as their previous roles. In Britain job loss usually means a worse job elsewhere.

Too many employers focus on extracting quick profits from cheap and flexible labour. An alternative approach is to embrace worker representation on boards, creating workplace democracy. We need to restore dignity and security at work, while recognizing jobs will become more flexible. Establishing worker bargaining power and rights in a fairer, but competitive, labour market is the key. Taking the route to better, more productive jobs need not be with trade unions on board. The union movement has had a mixed record in finding productive deals with employers. Employers should be required to offer parity in pay and benefits for subcontracted workers – including training and where possible progression pathways.

The Government could do more to encourage a longer view among businesses.[12] This could include incentives and rewards for companies investing in retraining and reskilling alongside research and development. The distinction between the workplace and the classroom will be increasingly blurred. It is about giving people the skills and pathways to progress, and to train in their chosen careers.

Paying Decent Wages

It is also about paying decent wages. Stagnating and falling real wages are causing serious problems. This is not only about the national minimum wage, the most frequently discussed policy lever, but the salaries expected for those contributing an essential public good. We could be more transparent about which employers pay more for their employees.

We have got used to the chasm between the pay of chief executives, bankers and finance directors and the salaries of 'average' workers. Yet it says much about modern British society that no one blinks when figures reveal that teachers, nurses, social workers, paramedics and police officers earn much less than train and tram drivers, rail repairers and waste disposal operatives.[13] Many of the country's key public service workers, with dwindling economic capital, have been consigned to a lower-class status.

The burning question is how can the country break free from the real wage squeeze of the past ten years? Inclusive growth requires workers across the entire pay distribution to get a fair share of the available 'rents', or excess profits. Backward-looking arguments for returns to the days of well-paid manufacturing jobs serving local labour markets are redundant. Workers' bargaining power has diminished in advanced countries – not just through the loss of collective bargaining, but also through the rise of insecure working arrangements and outsourcing, together with less structured company pay grades. Productivity has been decoupled from median earnings: since 1990, growth of the former has outstripped the latter, with respective 49 and 19 per cent increases in output per hour and median weekly earnings in real terms.[14] Stagnant pay highlights how the balance of power has shifted away from workers. This needs rebalancing: a reasonable ask in a world of rising corporate profits and a falling share of national income spent on wages.

These patterns are pronounced in 'superstar' technology companies.[15] Global organizations like Alphabet (Google), Amazon and Facebook spend proportionately less on their workforce not because they pay low wages, but because their stock market valuations and profits are enormous. They command monopoly power in a global economy where profits are shifted across international borders.

Regulators have failed to keep pace with these trends. To rethink education and work we will need to consider their drivers: technical change (including automation, artificial intelligence and robotics), globalization, the demand and supply of skills, the market for workers, the market for final products offered to consumers, as well as the way these markets are regulated. Understanding and harnessing the multiple forces shaping the modern labour market is the path to inclusive growth and increasing wages.

Rethinking Education

In his 1958 book *The Rise of the Meritocracy* Michael Young predicted that a detached ruling class would be the ultimate consequence of the new grammar school tests developed in the 1950s. Young feared the new tripartite school system (grammars, secondary moderns and technical schools) would give superior status to academic skills over creative or technical ones. Schools and universities would sieve people according to 'education's narrow band of values' – picking out the best performers in academic tests. 'Education has put its seal of approval on a minority,' wrote Young, 'and its disapproval on the many.'

In reality most grammar schools would be abolished in England during the 1970s, but Young's prophetic warnings have been uncannily prescient: Britain's education system has placed ever-increasing emphasis on academic testing. As we have seen, this is a manufactured race where the winners and losers can be predicted from the moment they are born. The tragedy is that the system has ended up labelling young people with other talents – creative, vocational and technical – as failures.

The core assembly-line model of education has changed little since Victorian times. Children are taught in traditional subjects and exams assess pupils' rote learning and memorization skills. Schools have become little more than exam factories in the face of unrelenting pressure to perform well in public league tables. There is little time for developing children's life skills, technical know-how or creative thinking. Education has been stripped down to one aim: teaching to the academic test. 'Memorizing formulas, essays, quotes and all that is required by exam boards for twenty-eight exams in four weeks is not preparing us for the future,' complained one sixteen-year-old pupil after completing her examinations in 2017.[16] Just as Young predicted, we have created an academic sorting machine: selecting talent on a narrow set of metrics which have questionable real-world relevance for many students.

The central insight from education's ever-escalating arms race is that education in Britain operates as a positional good. What matters is not the school or university qualifications you acquire but how superior they are compared with what others have achieved. Our education system mirrors the hierarchical class culture it originates from. Children's school results reveal who ranks the highest, not who has been prepared for later life.[17] And pupils from poorer backgrounds are hopelessly ill-equipped to compete with their more privileged peers.

We have become hyper-selective: seeking ever finer ways and grades to distinguish between the very highest academic achievers. The unintended consequences for large numbers of children who are not so academically inclined are dire: in 2017 England's school test reforms labelled a third of fifteen- and sixteen-year-olds failures for not reaching national benchmarks in English and maths. Most would be forced to resit the exams and three-quarters would be doomed to fail again.[18]

Academic success is increasingly a measure of how much support children receive, not how much talent or potential they have. Children who score highly in cognitive tests in their early lives from lower-social-class or less-educated parents are less likely to achieve the same education levels reached by similarly able children from higher-social-class or better-educated parents. 'Even high ability children are unable to transcend the effects of their social origins,' researchers concluded. 'The problem of "wastage of talent" remains; young people from disadvantaged backgrounds are still lacking the opportunity to fully realize their potential within the British educational system.'[19]

Laudable aspirations to narrow the average academic attainment gap between poor children and their more privileged peers are doomed to failure. It has become a rigged race. Mechanisms are needed to unrig and reframe education as a system offering opportunities for all. Britain is consistently average in global league rankings based on academic tests.[20] But when comparing how well young people apply knowledge to solve problems in the real world it comes bottom of the heap.[21]

England has three times the proportion of low-skilled teenagers than the best-performing countries like Finland, Japan, South Korea and the Netherlands. The international evidence suggests other countries are better at equipping children with the basics required to get on in life. Functional maths and English can be taught as part of a practical, meaningful jobs-focused curriculum which encompasses key social skills. A properly thought-out, well-designed policy for lifelong learning, however, needs to start at age 3, not 14 or 16. The goal of education is not solely a quest to identify the best academic minds (important as this is), but to be the enabler of all talents.

We have lost sight of what education is for. It says much that former Education Secretary Ken Baker has performed a spectacular U-turn in his thinking on what schools should teach. Baker was the architect of the 1980s curriculum, testing and inspection regime that shapes England's schools to this day. But he became convinced that fourteen-year-olds should instead pursue distinct pathways suited to their particular talents: liberal arts; technical subjects; sports and creative arts; as well as a career strand. Such a move, he argues, could make future generations more employable and meet skill shortages.[22]

Education remains an uncertain journey for the half of the population pursuing a different path to the well-trodden 'royal route' to university. 'If at first you don't succeed, you don't succeed,' rued Helena Kennedy, revealing the lack of clear pathways for learners in poorly funded further education colleges. Kennedy dared to dream of creating a 'climbing frame of opportunity' for ongoing learning for part-time and mature students that linked colleges, schools and universities.[23] If poorly funded further education colleges are not part of the solution then they are part of the problem – current training at these colleges does not always match the skill needs of employers.[24]

A valid vocational pathway need not mean a drop in status or education standards. One suggestion is to trial the Asian method of delivering academic content to pupils through real-world problems.[25] This may prove to be more useful preparation for the new technological workplace. Academic snobbery is the main obstacle to change – a misguided belief that technical education is about 'shabby premises and dirty jobs down in the town'.[26] Ministers argue that academic streams should not be the exclusive preserve of posh pupils. Yet this logic has drifted into the flawed assumption that all children should pursue an academic education.

We need a rethink. Improved education systems – in particular enhanced cognitive skills – lead to stronger national economic growth, and more absolute mobility.[27] People get more productive when their brains work better. This is likely to be even more the case for Britain's workplaces and classrooms in the global economy of the twenty-first century.

Education's Hard Slog

Two universal lessons emerge from the evidence on how to fulfil education's promise as a lever of social mobility: always pursue quality over quantity and never compromise on costs. This holds true whether talking about teachers, early years education, apprenticeships or jobs. It is the recurring message from robust research undertaken in the United States and more recent trials published in Britain. Scrimping does not work. And scaling up is hard to do.

Nobel prize-winning economist James Heckman has demonstrated the benefits of quality pre-school investments that reduce the need for costly catch-up programmes later in children's lives.[28] The evidence comes from just two randomized control studies carried out in the United States – the Abecedarian and Perry experiments.[29] These have tracked the outcomes of small samples of disadvantaged children who benefitted from two pre-school programmes, the Perry Preschool Project and the Carolina Abecedarian Project, in the 1970s.

Much of the gains from these pre-school efforts relate to reduced crime rates later in life, rather than improved cognitive scores.[30] The Perry programme did not boost the long-term IQ of the children who participated, but it did create persistent improvements in personality traits: children were found to be less aggressive and anti-social, for example. Researchers believe these improved life skills in turn led to improved performance in later school tests, and better job and health prospects.

These were intensive, expensive programmes; in the Perry Project, qualified teachers were deployed in small classes and undertook weekly home visits. In Britain, larger scale, less intensive early years programmes like Sure Start centres have so far produced disappointing results.[31] A lack of qualified teachers continues to be the stumbling block to creating an effective early years education system.[32]

The same can be said for schools in general. Teachers – and their classroom teaching – are the most important factor within schools impacting on children's progress. They are the ones who can lift the attainment of poorer children.[33] International comparisons suggest that a strong teaching profession is a key ingredient of high-performing education systems.[34]

The problem is that improving teaching is a hard, unglamorous slog. It's too tempting for politicians to focus instead on fast but flawed fixes: new types of schools and ever more intricate ways of holding schools to account. And while we know teaching quality matters most, we have little knowledge of how to improve it.[35] There is greater variation in teacher quality within schools than between schools. And often our best teachers serve our most privileged pupils.

We are still grappling with education's seemingly intractable challenges: finding effective programmes to improve classroom practice and promote learning between teachers.[36] We don't know how to get teachers working in the places they are needed most: schools and further education colleges serving the country's mobility coldspots. One thing is certain: teachers are among the key public sector workers who warrant higher salaries and greater social housing subsidies in expensive cities such as London.

The school improvement movement can also cite its own success stories: charismatic head teachers who have turned around failing schools, new models that have transformed child outcomes, cities like London that have bucked national trends. But they all fail the hardest test of all: making a permanent difference across the nation as a whole.

Even when teachers are aware of what works best in the classroom, they don't necessarily act on it. Two-thirds of school heads said they use an accessible guide that suggests the best education bets based on reviews of worldwide evidence.[37] Yet surveys reveal that few schools actually adopt these cost-effective approaches (all focused on improving teacher–pupil interaction).[38] Old habits die hard.

The scale-up challenge has also emerged in the attempts to turn around lives by combining social and health community services alongside school reforms. The driving idea behind the Harlem Children's Zone (HCZ) is that the worlds outside and inside schools are deeply intertwined – echoing the evidence from America's social mobility map. Its founder, educator and social activist Geoffrey Canada, was convinced that a try-it-all approach was required to create a tipping point for a whole community.[39]

When Canada first established the Zone in a single block

in Harlem in 1994, his mission was ambitious: that every child in one of America's poorest districts would graduate from college. Two decades on from its creation the Zone's 'cradle-to-career' services help more than 8,000 children and 6,000 adults across nearly 100 blocks in Harlem.[40] They cover financial and legal advice; medical, nutritional and fitness services; asthma and obesity reduction initiatives; substance abuse treatment; parenting programmes, college counselling and job training. Hundreds of children also attend two Promise Academies from the age of three. The schools aspire to the highest standards of education, with frequent feedback to teachers, a longer school day, and a culture of high expectations.

Given the evidence that social mobility is influenced by factors inside and outside schools at a local level, the Harlem Children's Zone is an important test case to determine whether a community can be turned around. So far the results have been mixed. On the plus side, the maths achievement gap between some black children in the Promise Academies and the average for white students in New York disappeared. Such gains are unheard of in education.[41] Yet other children benefitting from the community interventions but not attending the academies failed to produce such impressive achievement gains.[42] It is too early to judge whether the Harlem Children's Zone will enable its students to attend college.[43]

Inspired by Canada's efforts, the Obama administration launched seven new 'Promise Neighborhood' initiatives to replicate the Harlem Children's Zone in other American cities.[44] Yet their budgets and ambitions fell well short of the levels in New York.[45] The problem was that the costs of the programme are unimaginably high by school reform standards.[46] Few expect the results of Harlem to be replicated. The message is that lives cannot be turned around on the cheap.

For Promise Neighborhoods in the US read Opportunity Areas in Britain. Established in social mobility coldspots, these are Government-supported local partnerships between schools, universities, businesses, charities and others. The aim is 'to ensure all children and young people have the opportunity to reach their full potential'.[47] But the programme was launched in 2017 against a backdrop of the first real-term cuts in schools funding in England in a generation. The evidence from both sizes of the pond suggests that if we have high ambitions for education to help improve social mobility amid growing inequality, then we must be prepared to pay for it.

CHAPTER 9

Unlocking
the Elites

IMPROVING RELATIVE MOBILITY

Opportunity Hoarders

Opportunity hoarding is the term first coined by American sociologist Charles Tilly to describe the tactics deployed by better-off families to prevent their children sliding down the social ladder and being overtaken by upstarts from below.[1] He observed an uncomfortable truth: social elites will do anything to avoid downward mobility. And in the zero-sum game of relative social mobility, that means preventing someone else from rising up. Gaining advantage in the system is observed in school and university admissions and job recruitment – anywhere hoarders can get ahead.

Opportunity hoarding is one of the core behaviours creating inequalities in society according to Tilly. It is not just elites who engage in hoarding but immigrant groups establishing a foothold in a new country. In his book *Durable Inequality* Tilly describes how successive waves of Italian-American migrants arriving in Long Island in the United States excluded other groups from certain occupations and business sectors. Exclusive networks are common among immigrant communities, but opportunity hoarding becomes even more divisive when enacted by powerful in-groups at the top of society that are hard for others to penetrate.

Keeping the working classes in their place has a long

history. In the novel *Jude the Obscure* by Thomas Hardy, Jude's efforts to get into Christminster, Hardy's fictional name for Oxford, are met with stiff resistance because of his lowly status. 'You will have a much better chance of success in life by remaining in your own sphere and sticking to your trade,' the Master of Christminster's Biblioll College advises Jude. Entry to Christminster (as with Oxbridge at the time) required the study of classical Greek and Latin texts. But this was offered exclusively at elite private schools, unavailable to the likes of Jude.[2] Hardy's tale of frustrated ambitions is an observation of opportunity hoarding in Victorian times. Today the hurdles to Oxbridge entry for outsiders are subtle but still significant: navigating a baffling system of nearly seventy colleges, each with their own traditions, preferences and idiosyncrasies, preparing for extra bespoke subject tests and submitting compelling personal statements. If we could invent a system that is eminently gameable by the middle classes and alienating to those not in the know then Oxbridge is surely it.

Gaining entry into the elite club requires more than academic credentials or mere money. You need to talk, look and behave in a certain way – as the Beckhams have learned in the early twenty-first century. It was always thus. In the mid-nineteenth century new moneyed industrialists from lowly beginnings resorted to self-help guides, with titles such as *How to Behave* and *Hints from a Gentleman*. 'Here you would find everything you needed to know: when to shake hands; how to bring a conversation politely to an end; how to sit and stand gracefully.'[3]

The global financial elite of the twenty-first century seek social status just as their forebears did two centuries before.

Hedge-fund billionaires climb the hierarchy through high art: sponsoring exclusive art galleries and museums, attending international opera festivals and investing in philanthropy. Getting on requires good taste.

Those at the top devote incredible resources to ensure their offspring do not fall through society's glass floor – even if they are missing the natural talent or work ethic that their lofty positions would have required otherwise. In societies with high inequality, the loss in income from slipping down the hierarchy is more severe, making parents anxious about their children's futures. It is an example of the powerful incentives of loss aversion.[4]

In reality, it takes a lot to fall down the ladder. Finding any good and clear representative examples of downward mobility is hard. Whilst anecdotal in nature, a colourful exception is Frederick Hervey, the seventh Marquess of Bristol.[5] He inherited a fortune estimated at £35 million. His largesse included oil wells in Louisiana and a large sheep farm in Australia. But he had a chronic drug addiction and died penniless. A slew of salacious news stories charted Hervey's spectacular fall from grace.[6]

In Britain 'unmeritocratic' factors restrict downward mobility, researchers claimed after scrutinizing the outcomes of low-attaining children born in 1970 from advantaged backgrounds.[7] The children retained their high status despite their lack of raw talent, which otherwise would predict more lowly positions. High-attaining children from less advantaged backgrounds meanwhile were unable to climb the social ladder, since there was no space on the rungs above to advance onto.

A parallel study in the United States found similar evidence of opportunity hoarding. A large proportion (43 per cent) of Americans in higher-income households were 'of modest skill'. Lower-income Americans with the skills and drive to get into the higher-income bracket in later life had a 42 per cent greater chance of making it if they had a college degree: 'From a mobility perspective, it would be better if college slots currently taken up by modestly skilled kids who remain at the top were filled instead with the smart, motivated kids who remain stuck at the bottom.'[8] It's easy to see why low social mobility damages a country's economic productivity: wasted talent costs dearly.

In *Dream Hoarders*, Richard Reeves has resurrected Tilly's arguments and charted how the upper middle classes in America are pulling away from the rest of American society by accessing the best quality education, housing, healthcare, and other services. According to Reeves, American hoarders are found among those in the top 20 per cent of incomes – a much wider group than the super-wealthy elites. 'Those at the top of the income ladder are becoming more effective at passing on their status to their children, reducing overall social mobility,' he argues.[9] Taken in isolation, nudging your daughter into a better college or helping the son of a professional contact to an internship may seem harmless. But Reeves argues the individual choices made by opportunity hoarders exert a cumulative effect on society as a whole, diminishing opportunities for non-elites.[10]

But it's often a fine line between the unscrupulous behaviour of school admission cheats and the actions of decent parents anxious to ensure their children don't suffer in a poorly performing school. In Britain at least, the middle classes are more worriers than warriors. Opportunity hoarding tends to be at its ugliest at the highest apex of society where resources are plentiful, places are few and competition is fierce.

Accusations of hypocrisy lie in wait for those who dare to take the moral high ground. The life-defining decisions parents make can set off family rifts and recriminations that reverberate across the generations. The son of the renowned theatre director and avowed socialist Jonathan Miller made the headlines when he publicly criticized his father for having sent him to a local state school. William Miller told the *Sunday Times* that his father's high-minded ideals had 'turned out to be a cavalier social experiment that saw all three of his children fail to gain a single qualification'.[11]

William would avoid taking the same risks with his own children, sending his two daughters to private school. A few years later the story took another twist. The *Sunday Times* revealed that Jonathan had contributed to his (other) grandchildren's private school fees and had felt ashamed for doing so. Local schools, he bemoaned, just didn't have that 'lustre and prestige' guaranteeing entry to Oxford and Cambridge. Educated himself at the prestigious independent St Paul's School, he lamented the fact that the privileged in society could 'afford to wrap their children in all sorts of protective educational devices which guarantee that they will become like their parents'. The 78-year-old added that he was 'quite pleased to think he hasn't got to see much more of this increasing malignant unfairness'.[12]

Awkward Climbers

Raising relative social mobility is hard to do. For politicians it is an uncomfortable aim, raising the unpopular prospect of creating losers as well as winners. For a person to rise up, there must be another who slips down society's ranks. 'This could create economic instability and social tensions,' cautioned an internal memo to Tony Blair and his Cabinet in 2001 when the Labour Government was aspiring to create a more open and meritocratic Britain. 'The losers would have no one to blame for their circumstances but their own lack of ability and commitment. This could create a lot of unhappiness and resentment.'[13]

It is a hard sell – even for those lucky enough to climb up the social ladder. In her book *Respectable*, Lynsey Hanley describes the 'risky, lonely journey' undertaken from the 'respectable working class' to the middle class.[14] 'Changing class is like emigrating from one side of the world to the other, where you have to rescind your old passport, learn a new language and make gargantuan efforts if you are not to lose touch with the people and habits of your old life,' Hanley writes.[15] Others who have made the climb say they suffer from imposter syndrome in their newly found positions of power.[16]

These accounts chime with the international evidence suggesting the upwardly mobile are not always happier than those 'suffering' less mobility.[17] Unhappiness may drive 'frustrated achievers' to seek change, and their expectations heighten as they become better off. Change and uncertainty are linked to lower levels of well-being.

Acquiring the education, skills and stable employment necessary for upward mobility brings higher levels of stress. This can lead to unhappiness. At the same time people who perceive genuine prospects of upward mobility in society are happier and more likely to make investments in their own and their children's future.

Social climbers often sacrifice other things in life. Upwardly mobile fifty-year-olds from the 1958 birth cohort study were refreshingly modest about their success when interviewed. One high-flying senior accountant explained that for all his professional success he had failed to form a long-term relationship: 'I've got a good job, good income and yet I'm still jealous of people that are earning a tenth of what I've got that are happily married with two kids, you know, or a . . ., I haven't got that side of life.'[18]

Hanley draws much of her inspiration from Richard Hoggart's *Uses of Literacy*, published sixty years previously in 1957. The book described the 'uprooted and anxious' working classes in middle-class settings, epitomized by the 'scholarship boy' uncertain of his place in elite university life.[19] Hoggart imagines a working-class student navigating an alien world of academe, with all its tacit middle-class rules and assumptions. His account still resonates with the unsettling experiences of many students entering the ancient quads of Oxbridge today.

But advocating more upward social mobility does not mean everyone should aspire to be rich or posh or go to Oxbridge. On the flipside, it does not mean everyone else should be deemed failures for pursuing other ways of leading successful lives. Campaigns to widen access into elite universities should be targeted at children from all back-grounds with the academic potential and interests that make that particular path right for them. Too often they slip into the lazy assumption that this particular aspiration should be for everyone.

Improving social mobility is about helping children who through no fault of their own have grown up with little chance of fulfilling their potential to make their own in-formed choices as to what they want to achieve. It is then down to their individual talents, hard work – and luck – to progress in the direction they have chosen. We can only hope that social mobility ensues when more opportunities are cre-ated. As the sociologist John Goldthorpe has argued, 'I would push for more genuine equality of opportunity and then let the mobility chips fall where they will.'[20]

Smashing Through Glass Floors

When it comes to these frontline battles – where real lives are at stake – the consensus that social mobility is a good thing evaporates. Your view of it tends to depend on whether you are peering down or up the social ladder.

Prominent actors from working-class backgrounds, in-cluding Michael Caine, Helen Mirren and Julie Walters, have raised concerns that job insecurity and low pay during the critical early career years are making the creative in-dustries the preserve of the privileged elite. 'If I was start-ing out now, it would be a lot harder, because my parents could never have supported me through that "Is it going to happen?" period,' the actor David Morrissey told the *Radio*

Times. 'We're creating an intern culture – it is happening in journalism and politics as well – and we have to be very careful because the fight is not going to be there for people from more disadvantaged backgrounds.'[21]

Unpaid internships are the curse of the creative arts according to the former Arts Council chair Peter Bazalgette.[22] The Globe theatre, the British Museum and the TV show *The X Factor* have been berated for the exploitative practice. In 2013, nearly half (46.5 per cent) of Equity members working in theatre, and a quarter (25.1 per cent) working in film had taken unpaid internships and worked for free.[23] Campaigners advocate a complete ban.[24]

Not all actors share these views. Harrow-educated Benedict Cumberbatch has argued that thespian talent comes from all backgrounds: 'One of the best things about being an actor is that it's a meritocracy.'[25] Yet the point made by Cumberbatch's colleagues is that the barrier is one of access: getting a foot in the (stage) door in the first place to allow your talent to shine. Those from poorer backgrounds don't have the support and financial security to survive the time before they get their break.

Sixties singer Sandie Shaw suggested there is a systematic bias against working-class musicians. 'Finance is the biggest barrier for emerging artists,' she warned politicians. 'At the moment, unless you're Mumford & Sons and come from a public school and have a rich family that can support you, you're on the dole and you're trying to work and, by the time you get a sniff of a record contract, you just grab anything that they might offer you.' She argued it would be impossible for her, the daughter of a Dagenham car worker, to be successful now, and urged bankers and businessmen to invest in new creative talent.[26]

Others see no problem in millionaires paying tens of thousands at charity auctions to buy exclusive internships for their sons and daughters.[27] As prime minister, David Cameron made it clear that middle-class parents had every right to exploit their contacts to secure internships for their children.[28] Yet his deputy, Nick Clegg, launched a Government strategy to tackle the 'tacit conspiracy' of elite internships. 'A country that is socially mobile bases opportunity on your ability and drive, not on who your father's friends are,' argued Clegg. All work experience placements and internships within the civil service are now openly advertised rather than secured by word of mouth. Clegg argued: 'It should be about what you know, not who you know.'[29] Most people agree. Three-quarters of those surveyed supported a ban on unpaid work experience lasting more than four weeks.[30]

Levelling the Playing Field Through Lotteries

Loosening the iron grip the middle classes retain over the most sought-after state schools is contentious for the same reasons. This can lead to classic hoarding – securing the best education available at the expense of a less wealthy child. The highest-performing state schools, while below prestigious private schools in education's pecking order, are prized destinations for social climbers. They may only boost academic results marginally, but they can provide the social and cultural capital, networks and skills that can give an edge in the intense competition for places at elite universities and professions. Tinkering with selection criteria does not seem to work. Sharp-elbowed parents will always find ways to game admissions rules. They can (and do) buy a property close to the best schools or devote time to their local church just when it matters, or invest in private tutoring for their children. They will lie or cheat to get their child ahead.[31]

Lotteries for school admission offer a fair means of sweeping away middle-class advantages. Undeniably, the most equitable way to allocate places to equally deserving candidates at oversubscribed or selective state schools is to pick them randomly.[32] Yet as Phillip Collins, the *Times* journalist has quipped: 'A lottery, of course, is fair. That is why people hate them.'[33]

When asked about schools deploying random allocation to help decide which pupils they admitted, David Cameron responded that no child's education should be determined by 'the roll of a dice'. The irony is that many children's life prospects are damaged precisely because of the lottery of where they happen to be born and grow up. In the current system of school admissions the odds are stacked firmly against children from poorer backgrounds.

The 'roll of a dice' and unfairness arguments hinge critically on whether there is full uptake of school places and increased demand over and above the places available. Increasing numbers of schools are deploying ballots, alongside other admissions criteria, recognizing this is the fairest way to allocate places when they are oversubscribed.[34] When explained clearly there is more support for the idea among the general public than might be imagined.[35]

Selective Schools

The schools of choice for many opportunity hoarders are the academic hot houses – state grammars and selective independent schools. As we have seen, these exclusive schools continue to feed the country's elites. Brilliant education establishments many may be, but they are accessible only to the children of families who can afford to get in. Parents must pay for years of private tutoring to excel in entrance tests; for private schools there is the additional cost of substantial school fees.

For many of those who made it into grammars in the era of selective state secondary schools they were genuine engines of social mobility. And the surveys of leading people from medicine to politics, acting and even Nobel prizewinners, show the products of selective schools did indeed do extremely well: around a quarter to a third of the country's top people are former grammar-school boys and girls.[36]

But the experience of the grammar-educated minority contrasted with the majority of the population who did not make the grade. Three-quarters of children were labelled academic failures at age 11. A bigger gap between the wages of the highest and lowest paid people has been found for those born in areas of grammars compared with those from areas of comprehensive schools.[37]

There is a major drawback to introducing more grammars, whatever their impact was in the past. Poorer children already lag behind their more privileged peers by the end of primary school. Any new cadre of selective state schools would become exclusive schools for middle-class students – most likely lowering social mobility.

Intakes of the existing 163 grammars are highly skewed.[38] Less than 3 per cent of entrants to 'super-selective' schools are entitled to free school meals. Yet the average proportion of pupils entitled to free school meals in their immediate local communities is 18 per cent.[39] Poorer pupils with high marks have a 25 per cent chance of attending a grammar compared with the 70 per cent chance for similarly high-achieving better-off pupils.[40]

Grammars require a radical overhaul of admissions – incorporating random allocation of equally deserving candidates. Instead of trying to identify ever more intricate ways of distinguishing between candidates, the schools could agree a threshold of academic excellence that is good enough for entry. Those that pass the grade would then be randomly picked. Grammars might then help rather than hinder social mobility.

If there is an education topic more divisive than grammars, then it is private schools. Their enduring success in feeding Britain's elites coupled with their exclusivity make them as contentious as the class divide itself. The education apartheid that divides Britain's schools doesn't exist in similar countries, including Canada and Australia.

The education philanthropist and Sutton Trust founder Sir Peter Lampl advocates a radical way of opening up leading independent day schools: introducing means-tested fees – adopting a principle embraced by Ivy League colleges in the US.[41] This, he argues, would democratize selection at the schools, enabling children from all backgrounds to benefit from their teachers and facilities.

A trial at the Belvedere School near Liverpool (a former direct grant girls' grammar school that had turned independent when the local authority switched to a comprehensive system in the 1970s) not only found improved results, but at lower cost per pupil than if they attended state schools (for the girls who needed help with fees).[42] The evaluation showed that unfulfilled talent is out there, waiting to be developed. 'If we really want to break down the Berlin wall between state and independent schools Open Access is the answer,' Lampl has argued.[43] Yet paying for a fully blown 'Open Access' scheme – operating for around 100 leading independent day schools – is a difficult sell to Ministers on both sides of the political divide.[44] Labour politicians are opposed to more academic selection, while Conservative politicians are nervous of diverting state funding to the private sector, particularly when budgets are tight.

A more palatable approach for politicians (but still controversial) may be to demand that private schools form genuine and accountable partnerships with state schools or relinquish the charitable status they enjoy that saves them hundreds of millions of pounds in tax breaks each year.[45] The parallel with other 'for-profit' schools and universities operating in other countries is plain to see, given the profits made by private schools, much of which are reinvested back into the schools.

Fairer University Admissions

Deploying lotteries also offers a potential solution to the vexed issue of university admissions. Who wins degree places at the country's leading universities is a key battleground for relative social mobility: they remain the breeding ground for Britain's elites. Bombarded by thousands of A-grade candidates, the most sought-after universities are resorting to 'hyper selectivity' – ever more refined but unreliable ways of selecting the 'very best' academic talent. The truth is the admissions system for the highest-achieving school pupils, at highly selective universities like Oxford and Cambridge, is already a lottery.[46] It is just one masquerading as a highly sophisticated academic selection process.

The A and A* grades in A levels are not reliable enough measures for such intricate academic sorting. They are as much signals of how much preparation and support teenagers have received, as they are of pure academic talent and potential.[47] Exam grades are susceptible to how well students happen to do on the day and the varying judgement calls made by those marking tests. We must also remind ourselves what this academic selection is for: most graduates pursue non-academic careers after university, requiring a range of attributes and skills.

A university selection system not only fair, but fit for purpose, would identify a threshold of academic excellence and then select students randomly. One possibility would be to compensate losers in the lottery in some way – perhaps guaranteeing a place at another highly selective institution.

Another option, adopted by Dutch medical schools, is to select the very highest academic performers and enter lower achievers into a lottery.[48] Deploying random allocation alongside simple academic criteria would have the added benefit of cutting down on the escalating costs of admissions. The evidence suggests academic standards would be upheld.[49]

Yet another option is to create a British 'per cent' scheme following the model trialled by universities in Texas and California. This would guarantee a university place to, say, the top 10 per cent of academic performing pupils in each state school in a local region or across the country – irrespective of the actual grades they achieved. This would recognize the achievement of children in the context in which they grow up: getting to the top of the class in difficult circumstances means more than doing so in a highly supportive environment.[50]

The biggest impact of a per cent system could be to attract more middle-class pupils into state schools – a likely boon for social mobility in itself. As the journalist Peter Wilby has argued, the scheme 'would have the wondrous effect of encouraging the middle classes to spread their children through the school system, instead of continuing to shovel them into social ghettos.'[51]

Improving relative social mobility is never going to be easy. Powerful but pragmatic measures are needed to smash through glass floors and class ceilings. Randomly allocating equally deserving candidates to over-subscribed schools and universities is the only way of levelling the education playing field.

Multi-generational Mobility

British elites are persistent. But just how persistent is only now becoming apparent. Most studies focus on intergenerational social mobility – measuring the link between the characteristics of one generation and the next. But researchers are now turning to multi-generational trends, detailing the dynasties that have preserved power for hundreds of years.

Traditional wisdom says that wealth is squandered over three generations.[52] 'From clogs to clogs in three generations' is a Lancashire proverb from around 1700.[53] Similar sayings have been handed down the ages in countries as diverse as Japan, China and the United States.[54] In family-run businesses the work ethic that enabled the first generation to make their fortune would be lost by the third generation, who would fritter it all away.

The 'rule of three' was supported by the early academic literature on social mobility. Nobel prizewinner in economics Gary Becker and his co-author Nigel Tomes assessed income mobility trends and concluded that 'almost all the earnings advantages or disadvantages of ancestors are wiped out in three generations'. Their publication, 'On Human Capital and the Rise and Fall of Families', became a classic text for social mobility scholars.[55]

But in 2014 economic historian Gregory Clark reached a radically different conclusion. He used a novel technique to measure social mobility rates – tracking the status of people with rare surnames from medieval to modern England, comparing their positions in society to people with more common surnames.[56] The results yielded a gigantic beta – the measure of persistence over successive generations. Norman conquerors recorded as property owners in the Domesday Book, for example, were 16 times more likely than other names to enter Oxford or Cambridge universities in 1170. A millennium on, they were still 25 per cent more likely to do so.[57]

Clark's study is based on such small numbers that it is hard to generalize these patterns to the entire population. Yet the surname data offers tantalizing insights into the depth of aristocratic roots. Descendants of elites slip down to average status after ten or even fifteen generations, or 300 to 450 years. That's three times the generational persistence normally observed when using income, social class or education to measure status.

Some famous names feature in Clark's book *The Son Also Rises*. At least fifty-eight Pepyses – all related to the famous diarist Samuel Pepys – attended Oxford or Cambridge in the last 500 years, far more than would be expected for such a rare surname. Joseph Bazalgette, the Victorian civil engineer, was among the top 5 per cent of surnames associated with high wealth. His great-great-grandson, Peter Bazalgette, former chairman of Arts Council England, is now a vociferous campaigner for equal access into the creative arts.

David Cameron is a classic member of the tenth generational elite (but not mentioned in Clark's study since Cameron is a relatively common surname).[58] He is the ninth great-grandson of Sir Edmund Sawyer who served as an auditor for Prince Charles (later King Charles I) in 1623.[59] Cameron also descends from King William IV who ruled the country in the

1830s.[60] He also happens to be a distant relative to Boris Johnson.

David Beckham has a lot of catching up to do. But then he breaks with British tradition in so many ways – the tattooed working-class icon whose children rub shoulders with the young royals, the boy who left school to pursue an on-the-job training course who found worldwide fame, the son of a kitchen fitter who lifted himself into the most exclusive elites. According to Clark, Beckham is simply a 'happy accident' – one of the social climbers every generation gets by chance.

Clark finds that persistence in surname status is strikingly stable across several countries from Sweden, Japan and the United States to England; seemingly impervious to momentous societal changes over the centuries from the industrial revolution to the introduction of universal education and the modern welfare state, and even world wars. According to Clark, society (at least at the top) has remained immobile since records began. 'Lineage is destiny,' he asserts.[61]

Clark suggests that genetic transmission of 'social competence' – some underlying innate ability – is most likely to explain why elites remain unchanged over so many generations. 'By and large, social mobility has characteristics that do not rule out genetics as the dominant connection between the generations,' he argues. A review of Clark's book put it more boldly, concluding that it 'traffics in genetic determinism'.[62] It's not a new debate. Others have argued that current social mobility levels are the product of centuries of mating that has sorted out the genetically superior humans from the rest: the rich deserve their lofty positions in society because they are simply more able.[63] According to this argument we are a meritocratic society already, but we're uncomfortable with the unequal outcomes this has naturally created.

The complex interaction between children's environments and their genetic inheritance remains a hotly disputed area with an extensive scientific literature.[64] Twin studies and more recent quantitative genetics point to some genetic heritability in education and life outcomes.[65] Yet it's a gigantic leap from this to conclude that the upper social classes owe their status entirely to genetics, and that environmental factors play no part at all. Canadian economist Miles Corak argues:

> Powerful parents may influence child outcomes directly, rather than through inheritance, as a result of social institutions, and things like primogeniture, nepotism, access to select colleges, or lax wealth and estate taxation. A longstanding family culture may foster capacities to, for example, teach children to speak with a socially approved accent, buffer them from the downsides of health risks and other threats to their human capital, or simply to instil an identity of entitlement. A surname is not just an index of genes but also of social pressures and entitlements that keep some down and keep others from falling down.[66]

Moreover the economist Gary Solon concludes that there is no 'universal law of social mobility' as proposed by Clark, after an extensive review of all the evidence on multigenerational mobility.[67] Other studies focusing on particular groups in the population and those with particular surnames produce much smaller estimates of intergenerational persistence, or betas. Tracking surnames in his vast database of the American population, Chetty found around twice the levels of mobility Clark did. At the same time Solon questions the old assumption that persistence of wealth fades away after three generations. 'Just as recent research has found that the intergenerational income elasticity varies considerably across countries, we may find that multigenerational mobility behaves differently in different times and places,' he concludes.[68] In 2018 an OECD study estimated it would take descendents from low income families five generations to reach average income in the UK.[69]

Conclusions

The environment we live in shapes us. Britain's lower income mobility compared with other similar populations such as those in Australia and Canada indicates that outside forces in society can markedly influence the outcomes of our lives. 'Why am I the first Kinnock in a thousand generations to be able to get to university? asked the Labour Party leader Neil Kinnock during a Welsh conference speech in 1987. 'Was it because our predecessors were thick? Of course not. It was because there was no platform upon which they could stand.' Kinnock's son Stephen also went on to become a Member of Parliament after studying at Cambridge, and is now married to a former prime minister of Denmark. How many more families are waiting for the platform?

How else can we explain why thousands of students from the poorest backgrounds end up as high achievers when they are given the opportunity?[70] Similarly qualified state-educated medical students are, for example, almost twice as likely to finish in the top 10 per cent of final tests for medical graduates, compared with their independently educated classmates. 'One possibility is that once given equal access to resources, state-educated students take advantage of the opportunities available to them,' argued Professor Jen Cleland, who led the research.[71]

Yet the surname data we have discussed provides another indication that advantage and disadvantage at the extremes of society extend over a longer time period than just one generational jump. The study of multi-generational mobility is in its infancy, but few believe the 'rule of three' still applies: at the highest and lowest rungs of society's ladder our prospects are linked not just to the status of our parents but that of our great-great-great-grandparents. That is one of the central conclusions of this book.

The higher up Britain's social hierarchy you go, the stickier it gets. The Royals are strong contenders for the country's most immobile family. They have held on to power – apart from the occasional blip – for thirty-seven generations, spanning over 1,200 years.[72] That's generational persistence on a geological time frame. Today's monarchs are distant descendants of King Alfred the Great, who reigned in 871. Vast inherited wealth – including ancient castles and extensive estates – has enabled this country's aristocratic families to hoard opportunity over successive generations. Many landed gentry still rank among the richest people in the country, showing the new hedge-fund elites what staying power really means.[73]

The journalist Harry Mount explains that attending public schools – institutions as old as the family dynasties themselves – is also key to 'Why the Aristocrats Always Win'. 'Tim Nice-But-Dim rarely becomes Tim Poor-But-Dim,' Mount writes, acknowledging that high status is not always down to merit. 'If Tarquin is clever, he becomes a billionaire hedge-funder . . . Even if he's not so bright, he can become a perfectly adequate stockbroker.' Every direct male Mount ancestor for six generations has been to public school and Oxford. And not one of them has divorced – 'the quickest way to destroy an inheritance'.[74]

Amid the gaping wealth divide of the twenty-first century, elite family advantage is likely to extend over many generations into the future. Funds can be invested in financial and capital assets for the long term. Grandchildren and great-grandchildren will benefit long after the money has been set aside.

There is also a maturing force: the grandparent effect. The grey pound can make a big difference to the lives of grandchildren: paying for expensive school fees or handing down huge housing wealth. The odds of grandchildren becoming professionals rather than unskilled manual workers are at least two-and-a-half times better if the grandparents were themselves professionals.[75] This effect persisted even when parents' education, income, and wealth were taken into account. When time-poor parents are at the height of their busy careers, time-rich grandparents can step in to help with child-rearing duties.

Education's lost souls – the unskilled and unqualified – meanwhile are likely to be generational dynasties that go back not just fifty years, but centuries. In 1843 Charles Dickens observed children in London's prisons, warning they 'come of untaught parents, and will give birth to another un-taught generation'.[76] They were, in other words, the victims of intergenerational immobility: crippled by poor numeracy and literacy.

Dickens, himself a personal story of social mobil-ity, backed ragged schools, the inner-city academies of their day, set up by charities to provide free education for destitute children.[77] It all sounds remarkably similar to early twenty-first-century Britain. In the country's social mobility coldspots journalists have written about children growing up in households of 'trans-generational' unemployment where multiple generations of family have never worked.

The implication of future multi-generational persist-ence is far-reaching. It reveals just how much is at stake if we don't address Britain's social mobility problem. Failure to improve social mobility will leave a legacy for not just one or two but many generations to come. The problem will only magnify. On the other hand, one life transformed today can create a ripple effect that will enhance the lives of relatives far into the future.

It also prompts an unsettling question. Could it be that the post-war boom in social mobility was a historical one-off – a once-in-several-lifetimes blip in which education, in-clusive economic growth and greater equality happened to combine to improve opportunities at a time when the nation was in desperate need of replenishing its depleted pool of talent? Britain's golden age has given way to a dark age of shrinking opportunity: growing and multi-faceted inequal-ity, an escalating educational arms race amid falling absolute mobility.

The economic, social and political costs are mounting. Britain's poor productivity highlights the plight of millions of underpaid workers with little prospect of progressing up the career ladder. National political debate plunges into ever more polarized and populist extremes. The postcode you grow up in has a profound impact on your life prospects.

Areas of buoyant social mobility, across the world and here in Britain, however, offer rays of light and realistic aspirations to work towards. These are places where diverse aspirational and integrated communities enjoy affordable homes and benefit from good schools and dynamic industries investing in their workers.

Ideally the country should aim for higher levels of both absolute and relative intergenerational mobility. We need a world in which the nation's caravan is moving more quickly, particularly for those struggling at the back of the queue. We also need to allow people to leap ahead of others, through their hard work, talent – and a little luck. We need to confront the enemies of social mobility: the school admissions cheats and opportunity hoarders; the bad employers and socially selective schools; the detached elites and the ills of poor parenting and extreme inequality.

But we must also concede that we too are sometimes part of the problem. Have we ever stepped over the line – stretching the truth to ensure that our son or daughter gets that coveted school place displacing an equally deserving child from a family ill-equipped to compete in this education zero sum game? Are we loading expectations onto our children to pursue the high status university route when they are better suited to pursuing a less high-powered but more family-friendly career? In the relentless arms race of education it's easy to trample over the prospects of the less fortunate when fighting for the futures of own families and friends. Difficult as it is to stomach, we too are enemies of social mobility if we believe our own offspring should somehow be exempt from being downwardly mobile.

Britain needs a new model of social mobility: one that develops all talents, not just academic, but vocational and creative – and one that encourages people to fulfil their potential wherever they happen to be born. It is entirely possible to create a fairer education system, stronger economy and more equal society that, working together, would boost social mobility once again.

Notes

INTRODUCTION – THE TALE OF THE TWO DAVIDS

1. http://www.telegraph.co.uk/education/10699476/Michael-Gove-Number-of-Etonians-in-Camerons-cabinet-is-ridiculous.html.

2. For more on the cohort studies see H. Pearson (2016), *The Life Project: The extraordinary story of our ordinary lives*, Allen Lane. The author discusses in detail the history of the British birth cohort data, stating 'This is the tale of these studies and the remarkable discoveries that have come from them. Touching almost every person in Britain today, they are one of our best-kept secrets.'

3. It compares the earnings of males at age 42 in the year 2000 with the earnings of their parents when they were aged 16 in 1974. Females are not included in this analysis because so few worked in the first cohort and the sample size is therefore small.

4. https://www.thetimes.co.uk/article/the-sunday-times-rich-list-2017-boom-time-for-billionaires-pzbkrfbv2.

5. Our own calculations from the National Child Development Study which follows all individuals born in Britain in a week of March 1958 over time. Sons' earnings are measured at age 42 in 2000, and parental income when the cohort member was aged 16 in 1974.

6. Our own calculations from the British Cohort Study following all individuals born in Britain in a week of April 1970 over time. Sons' earnings are measured at age 42 in 2012, and parental income when the cohort member was aged 16 in 1986.

7. Tragically we do not have a national cohort study tracking life outcomes of those born in the 1980s, as the study was axed following Government funding cuts.

8. In other words, this compares the earnings of an individual at the 90th percentile (ranked 10 per cent from the top and therefore earning more

than the other 90 per cent of workers) with the earnings of workers at the 10th percentile (ranked 10 per cent from the bottom) in the earnings distribution.

9. Our own calculations from the 1980 and 1990 General Household Survey and the 2000, 2010 and 2017 Labour Force Survey. All full-time workers aged 25 to 64.

10. https://www.thetimes.co.uk/article/the-sunday-times-rich-list-2017-boom-time-for-billionaires-pzbkrfbv2.

11. https://www.moneyadviceservice.org.uk/en/corporate/a-picture-of-over-indebtedness https://www.moneyadviceservice.org.uk/en/corporate/one-in-six-adults-struggling-with-debt-worries.

12. Our own calculations, using data from the 2014 Wealth and Assets Survey.

13. T. Piketty (2014), *Capital in the Twenty-First Century*, Harvard University Press.

14. http://www.telegraph.co.uk/news/2017/02/07/david-beckham-has-given-hope-knighthood-near-future/.

15. http://www.economist.com/blogs/bagehot/2016/04/david-cameron-s-taxes.

16. Piketty (2014).

17. Samantha met David's sister at Marlborough.

18. https://www.allaboutschoolleavers.co.uk/news/article/229/david-beckham-and-other-famous-apprentices. Beckham attended Chingford High School in East London.

19. https://www.theguardian.com/football/blog/2013/may/17/david-beckham-alex-ferguson-manchester-united. At Manchester United he became renowned for the hard work and dedicated practice that made him one of the best free-kick specialists in the world.

20. https://en.wikipedia.org/wiki/Class_sketch.

21. They are: I – Higher-grade professionals, administrators and officials; managers in large industrial establishments; large proprietors; II – Lower-grade professionals, administrators and officials, higher-grade technicians; managers in small industrial establishments; supervisors of non-manual employee; IIIa – Routine non-manual employees, higher grade (administration and commerce); IIIb – Routine non-manual employees, lower grade (sales and services); IVa – Small proprietors, artisans, etc., with employees; IVb – Small proprietors, artisans, etc., without employee; IVc – Farmers and smallholders; other self-employed workers in primary production; V – Lower-grade technicians; supervisors of manual workers; VI – Skilled manual workers; VIIa – Semi-skilled and unskilled manual

workers (not in agriculture, etc.); VIIb – Agricultural and other workers in primary production. See http://www.encyclopedia.com/doc/1O88-Goldthorpeclassscheme.html.

22. G. Payne (2017), *The New Social Mobility: How the politicians got it wrong*, Policy Press.

23. M. Savage (2015), *Social Class in the 21st Century*, Pelican; M. Savage *et al.* (2013), 'A New Model of Social Class? Findings from the BBC's Great British Class Survey experiment', *Sociology* 47, 219–50. The seven classes are: elite; established middle class; technical middle class; new affluent workers; traditional working class; emergent service workers; precariat.

24. S. Dahou and J. Hamlin (2016), 'Ow Cockney is Beckham Twenty Years On? An investigation into H-dropping and T-glottaling', *Lifespans and Styles* 2, 20–27; http://www.manchester.ac.uk/discover/news/beckhams-getting-posher/.

25. http://press.conservatives.com/post/130746609060/prime-minister-conference-speech-2015.

CHAPTER 1: MOBILITY AND INEQUALITY

1. In the academic research arena, a lot of attention has been placed on how to use statistical modelling to obtain estimates of beta that are free from various biases. A careful discussion of these issues is contained in G. Solon (1999), 'Intergenerational Mobility in the Labor Market' in O. Ashenfelter and D. Card (eds.), *Handbook of Labor Economics*, North Holland Press.

2. http://cep.lse.ac.uk/about/news/IntergenerationalMobility.pdf. The underlying research was published as: J. Blanden, A. Goodman, P. Gregg and S. Machin (2004), 'Changes in Intergenerational Mobility in Britain' in M. Corak (ed.) *Generational Income Mobility*, Cambridge University Press.

3. *Sunday Times*, 26 July 2009.

4. https://www.gov.uk/government/organisations/social-mobility-and-child-poverty-commission.

5. HM Government, 'Opening Doors, Breaking Barriers'; https://www.gov.uk/government/uploads/system/uploads/attachment_data/file/61964/opening-doors-breaking-barriers.pdf.

6. https://www.gov.uk/government/uploads/system/uploads/attachment_data/file/622214/Time_for_Change_report_-_An_assessement_of_government_policies_on_social_mobility_1997-2017.pdf.

7. For international comparisons, see J. Blanden, (2013), 'Cross-national Rankings of Intergenerational Mobility: A comparison of approaches from economics and sociology', *Journal of Economic Surveys* 27, 38–73; M. Corak (2013), 'Income Inequality, Equality of Opportunity, and Intergenerational Mobility', *Journal of Economic Perspectives* 27, 79–102; O. Causa and A. Johansson (2010), 'Intergenerational Social Mobility', OECD *Economics Studies* 2010, 1–44. For income mobility changes in Britain, see J. Blanden, P. Gregg and L. Macmillan (2007), 'Accounting for Intergenerational Income Persistence: Noncognitive skills, ability and education', *Economic Journal* 117, C43–C60; J. Blanden, P. Gregg and L. Macmillan (2013), 'Intergenerational Persistence in Income and Social Class: The impact of within-group inequality', *Journal of Royal Statistical Society: Series A* 176, 541–63.

8. OECD, 'Intergenerational Transmission of Disadvantage: Mobility or Immobility across Generations? A review of the evidence for OECD countries'; http://www.oecd.org/els/38335410.pdf.

9. Numbers taken from Blanden (2011). UK number updated from J. Blanden and S. Machin (2017), 'Home Ownership and Social Mobility', Centre for Economic Performance, London School of Economics, Discussion Paper 1466.

10. This means if an adult earns £10,000 less than the average earnings for Britain as a whole, 35 per cent of this difference (£3,500) will be passed on to their children. In other words, the children will earn £3,500 less than the average for their own generation. In Denmark only 14 per cent of the relative difference is transmitted, on average, from one generation to the next. If a family earns £10,000 less than the average for their generation, their children will earn £1,400 less than the average.

11. See the methodological discussion of rank–rank correlations in M. Nybom and J. Stuhler (2016), 'Biases in Standard Measures of Intergenerational Income Dependence', *Journal of Human Resources*. Also see recent examples of evidence based on outcome ranks in population data from Denmark (S. Boserup, W. Kopzcuk and C. Kreiner (2013), 'Intergenerational Wealth Mobility: Evidence from Danish wealth records of three generations', unpublished paper, University of Copenhagen) and the United States (R. Chetty, N. Hendren, P. Kline and E. Saez (2014), 'Where is the Land of Opportunity? The geography of intergenerational mobility in the United States', *Quarterly Journal of Economics* 129, 1553–1623).

12. Sutton Trust (2012), 'The Social Mobility Summit'; http://www.suttontrust. com/wp-content/uploads/2012/09/st-social-mobility-report.pdf.

13. Ibid.

14. See Chetty's 2016 Lionel Robbins Lectures at the London School of Economics: http://cep.lse.ac.uk/_new/events/event.asp?id=291; this includes the chart in Figure 5.

15. Canada – M. Corak and A. Heisz (1999), 'The Intergenerational Earnings and Income Mobility of Canadian Men: Evidence from longitudinal income tax data', *Journal of Human Resources* 34, 504–33; Denmark –Boserup, Kopzcuk and Kreiner (2013); Great Britain – our own calculations from data in Blanden and Machin (2017); United States – Chetty, Hendren, Kline and Saez (2014).

16. The Stanford Center on Poverty and Inequality; http://inequality.stanford. edu/sites/default/files/SOTU_2015_economic-mobility.pdf.

17. Alan Krueger, 'The Rise and Consequences of Inequality', speech on 12 January 2012; https://www.americanprogress.org/events/2012/01/12/17181/ the-rise-and-consequences-of-inequality/

18. Interview with Alan Krueger, February 2017.

19. Numbers taken from Blanden (2013).

20. D. Andrew and A. Leigh (2009), 'More Inequality, Less Social Mobility', *Applied Economics Letters* 16, 1489–92.

21. R. Wilkinson and K. Pickett (2009), *The Spirit Level*, Penguin.

22. Interview with Alan Krueger.

23. Sutton Trust (2012), 'The Social Mobility Summit'; http://www.suttontrust. com/wp-content/uploads/2012/09/st-social-mobility-report.pdf.

24. Blanden and Machin (2017).

25. Ibid., based on calculations from the National Child Development Study (NCDS), which follows all individuals born in Britain in a week of March 1958 over time and the British Cohort Study (BCS), which follows all individuals born in Britain in a week of April 1970 over time. Children's owner-occupation (as adults) is measured at age 42 in 2000 for NCDS and at age 42 in 2012 for BCS.

26. T. Piketty (2014), *Capital in the Twenty-First Century*, Harvard University Press.

27. R. Chetty *et al.* (2016), *The Fading American Dream: Trends in absolute income mobility since 1940*, NBER Working Paper; http://www. equality-of-opportunity.org/assets/documents/abs_mobility_ summary.pdf.

28. L. Katz and A. Krueger (2017), 'Documenting Decline in US Economic Mobility', *Science*; https://d2ufo47lrtsv5s.cloudfront.net/content/early/2017/04/25/science.aan3264.full.

CHAPTER 2: RISING AND FALLING ECONOMIC TIDES

1. https://en.wikipedia.org/wiki/A_rising_tide_lifts_all_boats.
2. http://news.bbc.co.uk/onthisday/hi/dates/stories/july/20/newsid_3728000/3728225.stm.
3. N. Crafts (1995), 'The Golden Age of Economic Growth in Western Europe, 1950–73', *Economic History Review* 48, 429–47. In later work Crafts does note that whilst growth was relatively high in Britain in the 1950s and 1960s compared to later decades, the country fell behind competitor nations which grew much faster in the golden age period – see N. Crafts (2012), 'British Economic Decline Revisited: The role of competition', *Explorations in Economic History* 49, 17–29; N. Crafts and G. Toniolo (2010), 'Aggregate Growth, 1950 to 2005' in S. Broadberry and K. O'Rourke (eds.) *The Cambridge Economic History of Modern Europe*, Volume 2, Cambridge University Press.
4. See P. Armstrong, A. Glyn and J. Harrison (1984), *Capitalism Since World War Two*, Fontana.
5. http://www.songfacts.com/detail.php?id=7468.
6. https://en.wikipedia.org/wiki/God_Save_the_Queen_(Sex_Pistols_song).
7. Based on Annual Survey of Hours and Earnings numbers deflated by the consumer price index, used in P. Gregg, S. Machin and M. Fernandez-Salgado (2014), 'Real Wages and Unemployment in the Big Squeeze', *Economic Journal* 124, 408–32.
8. S. Machin (2010), 'Changes in UK Wage Inequality Over the Last Forty Years' in P. Gregg and J. Wadsworth (eds.), *The Labour Market in Winter*, Oxford University Press.
9. See C. Belfield *et al.* (2016), 'Two Decades of Income Inequality in Britain: The role of wages, household earnings and redistribution', *Economica* 84, 157–79.
10. Based on Annual Survey of Hours and Earnings numbers deflated by consumer price index used in Gregg, Machin and Fernandez-Salgado (2014).

11. R. Blundell, C. Crawford and W. Jin (2014), 'What Can Wages and Employment Tell Us about the UK's Productivity Puzzle?', *Economic Journal* 124, 377–407; J. Pessoa and J. Van Reenen (2014,) 'The UK Productivity and Jobs Puzzle: Does the answer lie in wage flexibility?', *Economic Journal* 124, 433–52.

12. Trades Union Congress (2014), 'UK Workers Suffering the Most Severe Squeeze in Real Earnings Since Victorian Times'; https://www.tuc.org.uk /news/uk-workers-suffering-most-severe-squeeze-real-earnings-victorian-times.

13. Gregg, Machin and Fernandez-Salgado (2014); http://touchstoneblog. org.uk/2016/02/now-a-lost-eleven-years-on-pay-never-before-know-in-history/.

14. Data taken from Office for National Statistics, https://www.ons.gov.uk/ employmentandlabourmarket/peopleinwork/labourproductivity/articles/ ukproductivityintroduction/jantomar2016.

15. Annual Survey of Hours and Earnings numbers deflated by consumer price index (CPIH from ONS), updated from Gregg, Machin and Fernandez-Salgado (2014).

16. Our own calculations – using data from the Family Expenditure Survey and Labour Force Survey.

17. A. Heath and C. Payne (2000), 'Social Mobility' in A. Halsey (ed.) *Twentieth Century British Social Trends*, Macmillan; J. Goldthorpe (1987), *Social Mobility and Class Structure in Modern Britain*, Clarendon Press; G. Marshall, A. Swift and S. Roberts (1997), *Against the Odds? Social class and social justice in industrial societies*, Clarendon Press; J. Goldthorpe and C. Mills (2004), 'Trends in Intergenerational Class Mobility in Britain in the Late Twentieth Century' in R. Breen (ed.), *Social Mobility in Europe*, Oxford University Press.

18. J. Goldthorpe and C. Mills (2008), 'Trends in Intergenerational Class Mobility in Modern Britain: Evidence from national surveys, 1972–2005', *National Institute Economic Review* 205, 83–100.

19. E. Bukodi, J. Goldthorpe, L. Waller and J. Kuha (2015), 'The Mobility Problem in Britain: New findings from the analysis of birth cohort data', *British Journal of Sociology* 66, 93–117.

20. Numbers taken from S. Clarke, A. Corlett and L. Judge (2016), 'The Housing Headwind: The impact of rising housing costs on UK living standards', Resolution Foundation.

21. https://www.theguardian.com/business/2016/jul/22/mike-ashley-running-sports-direct-like-victorian-workhouse.

22. *Good Work: The Taylor review of modern working practices*; https://www.gov.uk/government/publications/good-work-the-taylor-review-of-modern-working-practices.

23. Sutton Trust (2013), 'Real Apprenticeships'; https://www.suttontrust.com/wp-content/uploads/2013/10/APPRENTICESHIPS.pdf.

24. Sutton Trust (2017), 'The State of Social Mobility in the UK'; https://www.suttontrust.com/wp-content/uploads/2017/07/BCGSocial-Mobility-report-full-versioN_WEB_FINAL.pdf.

25. Sutton Trust (2017), 'Social Mobility and Economic Success'; https://www.suttontrust.com/wp-content/uploads/2017/07/Oxera-reporT_WEB_FINAL.pdf – This estimated an annual increase in the country's GDP of 2 per cent, equivalent to £590 per person or worth £39 billion to the UK economy as a whole; another report estimated that failing to improve low levels of social mobility would cost the UK economy up to £140 billion a year by 2050 – or an additional 4 per cent of GDP – http://www.suttontrust.com/newsarchive/140-billion-year-cost-low-social-mobility/.

26. The Gini coefficient measuring income inequality in Britain is 0.38, higher than the coefficient for Canada, at 0.34. On the other hand, were social mobility to worsen, and inequality fall to levels seen in the United States, the Gini coefficient would rise from 0.38 to 0.41; GDP per head would be lowered by 3.3 per cent.

27. http://voxeu.org/article/effects-income-inequality-economic-growth.

28. J. Stiglitz, (2013), *The Price of Inequality*, Penguin Books.

CHAPTER 3: MAPPING MOBILITY

1. Raj Chetty, Professor in the Economics Department at Stanford University; http://siepr.stanford.edu/scholars/raj-chetty.

2. http://www.sciencemag.org/news/2014/05/how-two-economists-got-direct-access-irs-tax-records.

3. R. Chetty, N. Hendren, P. Kline and E. Saez (2014), 'Where is the Land of Opportunity? The Geography of Intergenerational Mobility in the United States', *Quarterly Journal of Economics* 129, 1553–1623.

4. http://www.lse.ac.uk/website-archive/publicEvents/events/2016/10/20161024t1830vOT.aspx.

5. Chetty, Hendren, Kline and Saez (2014).

6. http://www.hbo.com/the-wire.

7. From the Equality of Opportunity Project, http://www.equality-of-opportunity.org/neighborhoods/ and Chetty, Hendren, Kline and Saez (2014).

8. http://www.the-american-interest.com/2012/08/10/down-to-the-wire/.

9. See the review of the early MTO work: http://www.nber.org/mtopublic/MTO%20Overview%20Summary.pdf.

10. R. Chetty, N. Hendren and L. Katz (2016), 'The Effects of Exposure to Better Neighborhoods on Children: New evidence from the Moving to Opportunity experiment', *American Economic Review* 106, 855–902.

11. http://www.nytimes.com/2015/05/04/upshot/an-atlas-of-upward-mobility-shows-paths-out-of-poverty.html.

12. Sutton Trust (2015), 'The Social Mobility Index'; http://www.suttontrust.com/researcharchive/mobility-map-background/.

13. Sutton Trust (2015), 'Mobility Map'; http://www.suttontrust.com/researcharchive/interactive-mobility-map/.

14. Even before primary school gaps are apparent: 72 per cent of disadvantaged children in the Lewisham Deptford constituency in South East London, for example, achieved a good level of development. This compared with only 19 per cent of five-year-olds reaching this benchmark in Kenilworth and Southam in Warwickshire.

15. https://www.theguardian.com/education/2017/jan/29/knowsley-education-catastrophe-a-levels-merseyside.

16. Sutton Trust (2012), 'The Social Mobility Summit'; http://www.suttontrust.com/wp-content/uploads/2012/09/st-social-mobility-report.pdf.

17. R. Putnam (2000), *Bowling Alone: The collapse and revival of American community*, Simon and Schuster.

18. R. Putnam (2016), *Our Kids: The American dream in crisis*, Simon and Schuster.

19. https://www.gov.uk/government/uploads/system/uploads/attachment_data/file/496103/Social_Mobility_Index.pdf.

20. http://www.telegraph.co.uk/education/2016/12/01/north-south-divide-good-secondary-schools-widening-warns-outgoing/.

21. A similar pattern had emerged for the areas most likely to vote for the anti-EU UK Independence Party in the 2015 general election. They had experienced lower wage growth than other areas of the country; http://www.ft.com/cms/s/2/fe5c6b4e-32f8-11e6-bda0-04585c31b153.html#axzz4DNFHTRsk.

22. British Social Attitudes survey; http://www.bsa.natcen.ac.uk/?_ga=1.3846397
    1.1565042058.1469308912.

23. https://www.gov.uk/government/news/state-of-the-nation-report-on-
    social-mobility-in-great-britain.

24. https://www.minneapolisfed.org/publications/the-region/interview-
    with-lawrence-katz.

25. http://www.nytimes.com/interactive/2016/11/08/us/politics/election-exit-
    polls.html.

26. http://abcnews.go.com/Politics/donald-trump-victory-similar-brexit/
    story?id=43420714.

27. With strong parallels to the Sutton Trust's constituency-level mobility
    index, the Social Mobility Commission subsequently produced its own
    index at local authority level in England; https://www.gov.uk/government/
    publications/social-mobility-index.

28. http://www.bbc.com/news/uk-politics-36616028.

29. Social mobility index from the Social Mobility Commission.

30. Our own calculations using official data on the Leave vote and the Social
    Mobility Commission's social mobility index.

31. https://www.gov.uk/government/speeches/britain-the-great-meritocracy-
    prime-ministers-speech.

32. http://www.nytimes.com/2016/11/08/us/politics/trump-rally.html.

33. https://www.theatlantic.com/business/archive/2014/11/
    why-its-so-hard-for-millennials-to-figure-out-where-to-live/382929/.

34. https://www.theatlantic.com/business/archive/2016/02/
    the-place-where-the-poor-once-thrived/470667/.

CHAPTER 4: THE EVER-ESCALATING EDUCATIONAL ARMS RACE

1. http://www.telegraph.co.uk/women/family/i-was-a-toxic-tiger-mum-
   but-ive-learnt-the-error-of-my-ways/.

2. Amy Chua (2011), *Battle Hymn of the Tiger Mother*, Penguin; http://
   battlehymnofthetigermother.com/the-book/.

3. http://www.tanithcarey.com/.

4. Sutton Trust (2015), 'Private Tuition Polling'; http://www.suttontrust.com/
   researcharchive/private-tuition-polling-2015/.

5. The main reason given was to help prepare for a specific test (cited by 52
   per cent of respondents). A similar number (47 per cent) said they had help
   with general school work.

6. P. Kirby (2016), 'Shadow Schooling: Private tuition and social mobility in the UK', Sutton Trust report, http://www.suttontrust.com/wp-content/uploads/2016/09/Shadow-Schooling-formatted-report_FINAL.pdf.

7. Ipsos MORI numbers, taken from Kirby (2016).

8. http://www.thelondonmagazine.co.uk/people-places/schools/the-rise-of-the-super-tutor.html.

9. https://www.vice.com/en_uk/article/super-tutors-are-earning-as-much-as-top-end-lawyers-729.

10. http://www.cherwell.org/2012/01/19/oxford-produces-supertutors/.

11. Russell Sage Foundation, 'Cross-National Research on the Intergenerational Transmission of Advantage'; http://www.russellsage.org/awarded-project/cross-national-research-intergenerational-transmission-advantage-crita.

12. J. Goldthorpe (2013), 'Understanding – and Misunderstanding – Social Mobility in Britain: The entry of the economists, the confusion of politicians and the limits of educational policy', *Journal of Social Policy* 42, 431–50.

13. http://www.publicfinance.co.uk/2007/03/admission-impossible-peter-wilby.

14. Sutton Trust (2017), 'Selective Comprehensives'; http://www.suttontrust.com/researcharchive/selective-comprehensives-2017/.

15. S. Gibbons and S. Machin (2003), 'Valuing English Primary Schools', *Journal of Urban Economics* 53, 197–219; S. Gibbons and S. Machin (2006), 'Paying for Primary Schools: Admissions constraints, school popularity or congestion?', *Economic Journal* 116, 77–92; S. Gibbons, S. Machin and O. Silva (2012), 'Valuing School Quality Using Boundary Discontinuities', *Journal of Urban Economics* 75, 15–28.

16. Ibid.

17. http://www.kcl.ac.uk/newsevents/news/newsrecords/2013/12-December/Almost-a-third-of-professional-parents-have-moved-home-for-a-good-school.aspx.

18. https://www.thetimes.co.uk/article/thanks-for-nothing-you-middle-class-scum-7z5fb5kjxb7.

19. http://archive.camdennewjournal.com/news/2014/apr/revealed-five-families-lose-school-places-after-admissions-fraud-investigations-0.

20. L. Feinstein (2003) 'Inequality in the Early Cognitive Development of British Children in the 1970 Cohort', *Economica* 70, 73–97.

21. Polly Toynbee, 'Childcare crisis', *Guardian*, 3 June 2003; https://www.theguardian.com/society/2003/jun/03/education.schools.

22. J. Jerrim and A. Vignoles (2013), 'Social Mobility, Regression to the Mean and the Cognitive Development of High Ability Children from Disadvantaged Homes', *Journal of the Royal Statistical Society: Series A (Statistics in Society)* 176, 887–906.

23. B. Bradbury, M. Corak, J. Waldfogel and E. Washbrook (2015), *Too Many Children Left Behind: The U.S. achievement gap in comparative perspective*, Russell Sage Foundation.

24. G. Schuetz, H. Ursprung and L. Woessmann (2008), 'Education Policy and Equality of Opportunity', *Kyklos* 61, 279–308.

25. F. Galindo-Rueda and A. Vignoles (2005), 'The Declining Relative Importance of Ability in Predicting Educational Attainment', *Journal of Human Resources* 40, 335–53.

26. https://opinionator.blogs.nytimes.com/2013/04/27/no-rich-child-left-behind/?_r=0.

27. https://www.timeshighereducation.com/features/robbins-50-years-later/2008287.article.

28. Sutton Trust (2008), 'NCEE Interim Report'; http://www.suttontrust.com/wp-content/uploads/2008/10/1NCEE_interim_report.pdf.

29. https://www.hesa.ac.uk/pr/4043-press-release-240.

30. https://www.offa.org.uk/wp-content/uploads/2006/07/OFFA-2014.01.pdf.

31. Our own calculations from the General Household Survey in 1980 and 1990 and the Labour Force Survey in 2000, 2010 and 2017.

32. 1981 and 1993 numbers based on the 1958 National Child Development Study and the 1970 British Cohort Study, taken from J. Blanden and S. Machin (2004), 'Educational Inequality and the Expansion of UK Higher Education', *Scottish Journal of Political Economy* 51, 230–49. The 2013 numbers are our own calculations from Understanding Society data (a national longitudinal study tracking data on 40,000 households over time).

33. J. Lindley and S. Machin (2016), 'The Rising Postgraduate Pay Premium', *Economica* 83, 281–306.

34. J. Lindley and S. Machin (2013), *The Postgraduate Premium: Revisiting trends in social mobility and educational inequalities in Britain and America*, Sutton Trust; http://www.suttontrust.com/wp-content/uploads/2013/02/Postgraduate-Premium-Report.pdf.

35. J. Lindley and S. Machin (2012), 'The Quest for More and More Education: Implications for social mobility', *Fiscal Studies* 33, 265–86.

36. S. Machin (2011), 'Changes in UK Wage Inequality Over the Last Forty Years' in P. Gregg and J. Wadsworth (eds.), *The Labour Market in Winter*, Oxford University Press.

37. M. Goos and A. Manning (2007), 'Lousy and Lovely Jobs: The rising polarization of work in Britain', *Review of Economics and Statistics* 89, 118–33; D. Autor and D. Dorn (2013), 'The Growth of Low Skill Service Jobs and the Polarization of the US Labor Market', *American Economic Review* 103, 1553–97.

38. D. Deming (2017), 'The Growing Importance of Social Skills in the Labor Market', *Quarterly Journal of Economic*, 132, 1593–1640.

39. P. Wakeling and D. Laurison (2017), 'Are Postgraduate Qualifications the "New Frontier of Social Mobility"?', *British Journal of Sociology* 68, 533–55.

40. Our own calculations from the General Household Survey in 1980 and 1990 and the Labour Force Survey in 2000, 2010 and 2017.

41. Goldthorpe (2013).

42. J. Britton, L. Dearden, N. Shephard and A. Vignoles (2016), 'How English Domiciled Graduate Earnings Vary with Gender, Institution Attended, Subject and Socio-Economic Background', Institute for Fiscal Studies, Working Paper W16/06; http://www.ifs.org.uk/publications/8233.

43. https://www.gov.uk/student-finance/new-fulltime-students.

44. https://www.hesa.ac.uk/pr/4043-press-release-240.

45. Department for Education, 'Widening Participation in Higher Education: 2016'; https://www.gov.uk/government/statistics/widening-participation-in-higher-education-2016.

46. http://www.docs.hss.ed.ac.uk/education/creid/Projects/34ii_d_ESRCF_WP3.pdf.

47. https://www.ucas.com/ucas/undergraduate/finance-and-support.

48. https://www.hesa.ac.uk/stats-dlhe.

49. Sutton Trust (2009), 'Innovative Admissions'; http://www.suttontrust.com/wp-content/uploads/2009/07/innovativeadmissions09.pdf.

50. Sutton Trust (2016), 'Oxbridge Admissions'; https://www.suttontrust.com/research-paper/oxbridge-admissions-undergraduate-widen-participation-contextual-data/.

51. Sutton Trust (2012), 'Student Survey'; http://www.suttontrust.com/newsarchive/debt-cost-worries-deterring-many-potential-students-survey/.

52. Sutton Trust (2012), 'Teacher Survey'; http://www.suttontrust.com/newsarchive/less-half-state-teachers-advise-able-pupils-apply-oxbridge/.

53. Sutton Trust (2012), 'The Personal Statement'; http://www.suttontrust.com/researcharchive/the-personal-statement/.

54. Sutton Trust (2008), 'NCEE Interim Report'; http://www.suttontrust.com/wp-content/uploads/2008/10/1NCEE_interim_report.pdf.

55. Sutton Trust (2015), 'Levels of Success'; http://www.suttontrust.com/wp-content/uploads/2015/10/Levels-of-Success3.pdf.

56. Sutton Trust (2014), 'Internship or Indenture'; http://www.suttontrust.com/researcharchive/internships/.

57. J. Jerrim and L. Macmillan (2015), 'Income Inequality, Intergenerational Mobility, and the *Great Gatsby* Curve: Is education the key?', *Social Forces* 94, 505–33.

58. D Laurison and S. Friedman (2016), 'The Class Pay Gap in Higher Managerial and Professional Occupations', *American Sociological Review*, forthcoming.

59. H. Steedman (2010), 'The State of Apprenticeship in 2010', Apprenticeship Ambassadors Network; http://cep.lse.ac.uk/pubs/download/special/cepsp22.pdf.

60. https://www.gov.uk/government/news/less-affluent-kids-are-locked-out-of-investment-banking-jobs.

61. R. Putnam (2016), *Our Kids: The American dream in crisis*, Simon and Schuster; http://www.simonandschuster.co.uk/books/Our-Kids/Robert-D-Putnam/9781476769905.

62. Sutton Trust (2014), 'Extracurricular Inequality'; http://www.suttontrust.com/wp-content/uploads/2014/09/Extracurricular-inequality.pdf.

63. Cabinet Office and Social Mobility Commission (2015), 'Social and Emotional Learning: Skills for life and work'; https://www.gov.uk/government/uploads/system/uploads/attachment_data/file/411489/Overview_of_research_findings.pdf.

64. A. Goodman, H. Joshi, B. Nasim and C. Tyler (2015), 'Social and Emotional Skills in Childhood and Their Long-Term Effects on Adult Life', Review for the Early Intervention Foundation; http://www.eif.org.uk/wp-content/uploads/2015/03/EIF-Strand-1-Report-FINAL1.pdf.

65. http://www.bbc.co.uk/news/education-38923034.

66. http://www.telegraph.co.uk/education/2017/08/31/government-orders-investigation-public-school-cheating-scandal/.

CHAPTER 5: EDUCATION'S LOST SOULS

1. The OECD's 2012 survey of adult skills: the Programme for International Assessment of Adult Competencies (PIAAC); http://www.oecd.org/site/piaac/. The example is a Level 2 question.

2. The OECD's Training Journal; https://www.trainingjournal.com/articles/
   news/british-youngsters-most-illiterate-developed-world-says-oecd.

3. K. Hansen and A. Vignoles (2005), 'The United Kingdom Education
   System in a Comparative Context' in S. Machin and A. Vignoles
   (eds.) *What's the Good of Education?: The economics of education
   in the* UK, Princeton University Press; A. Vignoles (2016), 'What
   is the Economic Value of Literacy and Numeracy? Basic skills
   in literacy and numeracy are essential for success in the labour
   market', IZA World of Labour 2016: 229; http://wol.iza.org/articles/
   what-is-economic-value-of-literacy-and-numeracy-1.pdf.

4. M. Kuczera, S. Field and H. Windisch (2016) 'Building Skills for All: A
   review of England', OECD Report; https://www.oecd.org/unitedkingdom/
   building-skills-for-all-review-of-england.pdf.

5. Department for Business Innovation and Skills (2012), 'The 2011 Skills
   for Life Survey: A survey of literacy, numeracy and ICT levels in England';
   https://www.gov.uk/government/uploads/system/uploads/attachment_
   data/file/36000/12-p168-2011-skills-for-life-survey.pdf#page=69.

6. Our own calculations from the OECD's PIAAC data, available at http://
   www.oecd.org/skills/piaac/publicdataandanalysis/#d.en.408927.

7. Our own calculations from the OECD's PIAAC data, available at http://
   www.oecd.org/skills/piaac/publicdataandanalysis/#d.en.408927.

8. OECD (2016), 'Building Skills for All: A review of England'; https://www.
   oecd.org/unitedkingdom/building-skills-for-all-review-of-england.pdf.

9. https://en.wikipedia.org/wiki/2011_England_riots#Suggested_
   contributory_factors.

10. https://www.gov.uk/government/speeches/michael-gove-to-the-
    durand-academy.

11. Department for Education (2015), '2010 to 2015 Government Policy:
    Academies and free schools'; https://www.gov.uk/government/
    publications/2010-to-2015-government-policy-academies-and-free-
    schools/2010-to-2015-government-policy-academies-and-free-schools [*sic*].

12. Gove would be removed from his position as Education Secretary by
    the Prime Minister, and his close friend, David Cameron. As minds at
    Conservative Party HQ turned to winning the next general election in
    2015, Gove's fate was sealed by private polling: he had become a toxic
    liability with teachers across the country; https://www.theguardian.com/
    politics/2014/jul/15/cameron-sacks-toxic-gove-promotes-women-
    reshuffle.

13. http://www.bbc.co.uk/news/education-37617616.

14. There were improvements in the proportion of pupils at age 16 attaining the expected benchmark of five GCSEs at grades A–C during the 1990s.

15. Speech at Ruskin College, Oxford, 16 December 1996; http://www.leeds.ac.uk/educol/documents/000000084.htm.

16. http://news.bbc.co.uk/2/hi/uk_news/education/6564933.stm.

17. S. Machin and S. McNally (2008), 'The Literacy Hour', *Journal of Public Economics* 92, 1441–62; S. Machin and S. McNally (2008), 'Gender and Student Achievement in English Schools', *Oxford Review of Economic Policy* 21, 357–72.

18. A. Adonis (2012), *Education, Education, Education: Reforming England's schools*, Biteback Publishing; A. Eyles, C. Hupkau and S. Machin (2016), 'Academies, Charter and Free Schools: Do new school types deliver better outcomes?', *Economic Policy* 31, 453–501.

19. Around 1.5 million children in state schools in England meet the eligibility criteria for free school meals. G. Whitty and J. Anders (2013), 'Narrowing the Achievement Gap: Policy and practice in England 1997–2010' in J. Clark (ed.) *Closing the Achievement Gap from an International Perspective*, Springer.

20. R. Lupton and S. Thompson (2015), 'Socio-economic Inequalities in English Schooling under the Coalition Government 2010–15', *London Review of Education* 13, 4–20.

21. G. Whitty and J. Anders (2014), '(How) did New Labour narrow the achievement and participation gap?', Centre for Learning and Life Chances in Knowledge Economies and Societies; http://sticerd.lse.ac.uk/dps/case/spcc/RN08GWJA.pdf.

22. Lupton and Thompson (2015).

23. BBC news website: http://www.bbc.co.uk/news/education-25187998.

24. Department for Education (2010), 'The Importance of Teaching'; https://www.gov.uk/government/uploads/system/uploads/attachment_data/file/175429/CM-7980.pdf.

25. Department for Education (2016), 'Educational Excellence Everywhere'; https://www.gov.uk/government/publications/educational-excellence-everywhere.

26. S. Higgins, D. Kokotsaki and R. Coe (2011), *Toolkit of Strategies to Improve Learning*, Sutton Trust; http://www.cem.org/attachments/1toolkit-summary-final-r-2-.pdf.

27. https://educationendowmentfoundation.org.uk/.

28. L. Dearden, S. McIntosh, M. Myck and A. Vignoles (2002), 'The Returns to Academic and Vocational Qualifications in Britain', *Bulletin of Economic Research* 54, 249–74.

29. Lupton and Thompson (2015).

30. https://www.gov.uk/government/publications/social-mobility-policies-between-1997-and-2017-time-for-change.

31. https://epi.org.uk/report/closing-the-gap/.

32. A. Wolf (2011), 'Review of Vocational Education – The Wolf Report'; https://www.gov.uk/government/uploads/system/uploads/attachment_data/file/180504/DFE-00031-2011.pdf.

33. http://www.jcq.org.uk/examination-results/gcses/2016.

34. These details are summaries taken from real school case studies.

35. J. Bynner and S. Parsons (2006), 'New Light on Literacy and Numeracy', NRDC report; http://dera.ioe.ac.uk/22309/1/doc_3186.pdf.

36. OECD (2016), 'Building Skills for All: A Review of England'; https://www.oecd.org/unitedkingdom/building-skills-for-all-review-of-england.pdf.

37. Our own calculations from the OECD's PIAAC data, available at http://www.oecd.org/skills/piaac/publicdataandanalysis/#d.en.408927.

38. A. Green, F. Green and N. Pensiero (2014), 'Why are Literacy and Numeracy Skills in England so Unequal? Evidence from the OECD's Survey of Adult Skills and other international surveys', Institute of Education, LLAKES Research Paper 47.

39. Bynner and Parsons (2006).

40. Department for Education (2016), 'Schools That Work for Everyone'; https://consult.education.gov.uk/school-frameworks/schools-that-work-for-everyone/supporting_documents/SCHOOLS%20THAT%20WORK%20FOR%20EVERYONE%20%20FINAL.PDF.

41. https://www.gov.uk/government/uploads/system/uploads/attachment_data/file/285990/P8_factsheet.pdf.

42. https://www.nao.org.uk/report/financial-sustainability-in-schools/.

43. R. Martin and H. Hodgson, with A. Maloney and I. Rayner (2014), 'Cost of Outcomes Associated with Low Levels of Adult Numeracy in the UK', Pro Bono Economics Report for National Numeracy; http://www.probonoeconomics.com/sites/probonoeconomics.com/files/files/reports/PBE%20National%20Numeracy%20costs%20report%202011Mar.pdf.

44. T. Newburn (2015), 'The 2011 English Riots in Recent Historical Perspective', *British Journal of Criminology* 55, 39–64; B. Bell, L. Jaitman and S. Machin (2014), 'Crime Deterrence: Evidence from the London 2011 riots', *Economic Journal* 124, 480–506.

CHAPTER 6: BRITAIN'S PRIVATELY EDUCATED ELITES

1. https://www.nationalgallery.org.uk/paintings/canaletto-eton-college.
2. https://en.wikipedia.org/wiki/Eton_College#cite_note-2.
3. G. Orwell (1941), *The Lion and the Unicorn: Socialism and the English genius*; http://orwell.ru/library/essays/lion/english/.
4. Sutton Trust (2012), 'The Educational Backgrounds of the Nation's Leading People'; http://www.suttontrust.com/researcharchive/the-educational-backgrounds-of-the-nations-leading-people/.
5. http://www.theguardian.com/politics/2014/mar/15/michael-gove-old-etonians-conservative-david-cameron.
6. Paul Weller on David Cameron's love for The Jam's 'Eton Rifles': 'Which Bit Didn't You Get?', *New Musical Express*, 25 April 2015; http://www.nme.com/news/music/paul-weller-12-1211374.
7. http://www.telegraph.co.uk/news/politics/conservative/11789390/Boris-Johnson-Tories-must-smash-down-barriers-to-social-mobility.html.
8. A. Reeves, S. Friedman, C. Rahal and M. Flemmen (2017), 'The Decline and Persistence of the Old Boy: Private schools and elite recruitment 1897–2016', *American Sociological Review*, forthcoming. The Clarendon schools are Eton, Charterhouse, Harrow, Rugby, Shrewsbury, Westminster, Winchester, St Paul's and Merchant Taylors'.
9. Sutton Trust (2012), 'The Educational Backgrounds of the Nation's Leading People'. 'The Arts' includes fine art, fashion, dance, museums and galleries.
10. Sutton Trust (2016), 'Leading People 2016'; http://www.suttontrust.com/researcharchive/leading-people-2016/.
11. http://www.telegraph.co.uk/news/politics/conservative/10439303/Truly-shocking-that-the-private-school-educated-and-affluent-middle-class-still-run-Britain-says-Sir-John-Major.html.
12. Social Mobility and Child Poverty Commission (2014), 'Elitist Britain', report, https://www.gov.uk/government/uploads/system/uploads/attachment_data/file/347915/Elitist_Britain_-_Final.pdf.
13. Sutton Trust (2012), 'Olympic Winners'; http://www.suttontrust.com/newsarchive/third-british-olympic-winners-privately-educated/.
14. Piers Morgan, 'The 100 British Celebrities Who Really Matter', *Daily Mail*, 12 March 2010; http://www.dailymail.co.uk/home/moslive/article-1255806/The-100-British-celebrities-really-matter-Piers-Morgan-10-1.html.

15. Sutton Trust (2014), 'Pathways to Banking'; http://www.suttontrust.com/researcharchive/pathways-banking/.

16. Sutton Trust (2016), 'Leading People 2016'.

17. Ibid.

18. Sutton Trust (2006), 'Educational Backgrounds of Leading Journalists'; http://www.suttontrust.com/researcharchive/educational-backgrounds-leading-journalists/.

19. http://www.thetimes.co.uk/tto/news/politics/article4651642.ece.

20. Sutton Trust (2010), 'The Educational Backgrounds of Members of Parliament in 2010'; http://www.suttontrust.com/wp-content/uploads/2010/05/1MPs_educational_backgrounds_2010_A.pdf.

21. Sutton Trust (2015), 'Parliamentary Privilege'; http://www.suttontrust.com/wp-content/uploads/2015/05/Parliamentary-Privilege-The-MPs-2015-2.pdf.

22. Sutton Trust (2016), 'Cabinet Analysis'; http://www.suttontrust.com/researcharchive/the-sutton-trust-cabinet-analysis/.

23. A. Giddens and P. Stanworth (eds.) (1974), *Elites and Power in British Society*, Cambridge University Press.

24. Sutton Trust (2006), 'Educational Backgrounds of Leading Journalists'.

25. http://news.sky.com/story/1671752/sheen-arts-becoming-harder-for-working-class.

26. D. O'Brien, D. Laurison, A. Miles and S. Friedman (2016), 'Are the Creative Industries Meritocratic? An analysis of the 2014 British Labour Force Survey', *Cultural Trends* 25, 116–31.

27. Sutton Trust (2014), 'Pathways to Banking'.

28. Cabinet Office (2016), 'Socio-economic Diversity in the Fast Stream: The Bridge report'; https://www.gov.uk/government/publications/socio-economic-diversity-in-the-fast-stream-the-bridge-report.

29. A. Halsey, A. Heath and A. Ridge (1984), 'The Political Arithmetic of Public Schools' in G. Walford (ed.), *The British Public School: Policy and practice*, Falmer Press.

30. http://www.isc.co.uk/media/3584/year_13_exam_results_2016_infographic.pdf. ISC schools educate about 80 per cent of the total number of private school pupils in the UK.

31. F. Njadi, J. Little and R. Coe (2016), 'A Comparison of Academic Achievement in Independent and State Schools', Centre for Evaluation and Monitoring, Durham University; https://www.isc.co.uk/media/3140/16_02_26-cem-durham-university-academic-value-added-research.pdf.

32. Sutton Trust (2011), 'Degrees of Success'; http://www.suttontrust.com/wp-content/uploads/2011/07/sutton-trust-he-destination-report-final.pdf.

33. There were only 130 free school meals pupils out of 16,110 Oxbridge students in total – whereas nearly half the intake came from independent schools; http://www.suttontrust.com/wp-content/uploads/2010/12/access-proposals-report-final.pdf.

34. Sutton Trust (2009), 'BIS Report'; http://www.suttontrust.com/wp-content/uploads/2009/07/BIS_ST_report.pdf.

35. Higher Education Funding Council for England, http://www.hefce.ac.uk/media/hefce/content/pubs/2013/201315/Higher%20education%20and%20beyond%20Outcomes%20from%20full-time%20first%20degree%20study.pdf; see also http://www.suttontrust.com/newsarchive/comprehensive-pupils-outperform-independent-grammar-pupils-university-degrees/.

36. F. Green, S. Machin, R. Murphy and Y. Zhu (2011,) 'The Changing Economic Advantage from Private Schools', *Economica* 79, 658–79.

37. Ibid.

38. L. Macmillan, C. Tyler and A. Vignoles (2015), 'Who Gets the Top Jobs? The role of family background and networks in recent graduates', *Journal of Social Policy* 44, 487–515.

39. Sutton Trust (2008), 'University Admissions by Individual Schools'; http://www.suttontrust.com/wp-content/uploads/2008/02/UniversityAdmissions.pdf.

40. L. Ashley, J. Duberley, H. Sommerlad and D. Scholarios (2015), 'A Qualitative Evaluation of Non-educational Barriers to the Elite Professions', Social Mobility and Child Poverty Commission report; https://www.gov.uk/government/uploads/system/uploads/attachment_data/file/434791/A_qualitative_evaluation_of_non-educational_barriers_to_the_elite_professions.pdf.

41. http://futurefirst.org.uk/blog/2014/07/04/future-first-david-laws-state-schools-missing-out-on-100m-of-alumni-donations/.

42. Former Prime Minister David Cameron, former Chancellor of the Exchequer George Osborne, former Mayor of London Boris Johnson and BBC journalist David Dimbleby are all former members; https://en.wikipedia.org/wiki/Bullingdon_Club.

43. http://life.spectator.co.uk/2015/09/etons-recipe-for-success/.

44. http://www.telegraph.co.uk/education/educationnews/11579752/Eton-head-Private-schools-too-expensive.html.

45. Sutton Trust (2016), 'Leading People 2016'.

46. R. Coe *et al.* (2014), *What Makes Great Teaching? Review of the underpinning research*, Sutton Trust; http://www.suttontrust.com/wp-content/uploads/2014/10/What-Makes-Great-Teaching-REPORT.pdf.

47. Independent Schools Council survey; http://www.isc.co.uk/media/2661/isc_census_2015_final.pdf.

48. http://www.etoncollege.com/CurrentFees.aspx.

49. http://www.ons.gov.uk/peoplepopulationandcommunity/personalandhouseholdfinances/incomeandwealth/bulletins/nowcastinghouseholdincomeintheuk/2015-10-28.

50. https://www.killik.com/search/?q=private+school; http://www.thisismoney.co.uk/money/news/article-2714121/The-cost-sending-two-children-private-school-As-fees-rocket-experts-advise-planning-early-applying-scholarships.html.

51. http://www.telegraph.co.uk/education/educationnews/11639293/Private-school-fees-at-their-least-affordable-since-the-1960s-research-shows.html.

52. http://www.spectator.co.uk/2013/11/five-star-schools/.

53. Sutton Trust (2010), 'Fee Remissions and Bursaries in Independent Schools'; http://www.suttontrust.com/wp-content/uploads/2010/07/finalbursariesreportstaffs.pdf.

54. https://www.gov.uk/government/uploads/system/uploads/attachment_data/file/347915/Elitist_Britain_-_Final.pdf.

55. M. Young (1958), *The Rise of the Meritocracy*, Pelican.

56. http://news.bbc.co.uk/2/hi/uk_news/162402.stm.

CHAPTER 7: THE WAY AHEAD

1. http://www.telegraph.co.uk/news/politics/london-mayor-election/mayor-of-london/10480321/Boris-Johnsons-speech-at-the-Margaret-Thatcher-lecture-in-full.html.

2. 'Minister Demands End to "Spiralling" Pay for University Chiefs', *Financial Times*, 21 July 2017; https://www.ft.com/content/5bed5b04-6c98-11e7-b9c7-15af748b60d0.

3. C. Young, C. Varner, I. Lurie and R. Prisinzano (2016), 'Millionaire Migration and Taxation of the Elite', *American Sociological Review* 81, 421–46; C. Young (2017), *The Myth of Millionaire Tax Flight: How Place Still Matters for the Rich*, Stanford University Press.

4. Speech by Iain Duncan Smith, Secretary of State for Work and Pensions (2010), 'Welfare for the 21st Century'; https://www.gov.uk/government/speeches/welfare-for-the-21st-century.

5. R. Chetty, N. Hendren and L. Katz (2016), 'The Effects of Exposure to Better Neighborhoods on Children: New evidence from the Moving to Opportunity experiment', *American Economic Review* 106, 855–902.

6. J. Waldfogel and E. Washbrook (2011), 'Early years policy', *Child Development Research* 1–12; J. Waldfogel (2006), *What Children Need*, Harvard University Press.

7. B. Hart and T. R. Risley (University of Kansas researchers) (2003), 'The Early Catastrophe: The 30 million word gap by age 3', *American Educator* Spring, 4–9.

8. https://www.nytimes.com/2017/09/03/upshot/to-understand-rising-inequality-consider-the-janitors-at-two-top-companies-then-and-now.html.

9. https://www.hesa.ac.uk/news/12-01-2017/sfr242-student-enrolments-and-qualifications.

10. http://oecdinsights.org/2014/12/09/is-inequality-good-or-bad-for-growth/.

11. Miles Corak, 'Social Mobility and Inequality in the UK and the US: How to slide down the *Great Gatsby* Curve'; https://milescorak.com/2012/05/22/social-mobility-and-inequality-in-the-uk-and-the-us-how-to-slide-down-the-great-gatsby-curve/.

12. R. H. Tawney (1931), *Equality*, Collins.

13. http://www.theguardian.com/commentisfree/2016/mar/13/decades-of-educational-reform-no-social-mobility.

14. http://news.bbc.co.uk/1/hi/uk_politics/7468506.stm.

15. https://scholar.harvard.edu/hendren/publications/fading-american-dream-trends-absolute-income-mobility-1940.

16. For US evidence on the decoupling of growth of median wages from productivity, see J. Bivens and L. Mishel (2015), 'Understanding the Historic Divergence between Productivity and a Typical Worker's Pay: Why it matters and why it's real', Economic Policy Institute; and A. Stansbury and L. Summers (2017), 'Productivity and Pay: Is the link broken?', paper presented at the Peterson Institute for International Economics conference on 'The Policy Implications of Sustained Low Productivity Growth', 9 November 2017. For evidence of decoupling from Britain, see P. Gregg, S. Machin and M. Fernandez-Salgado (2014), 'The Squeeze On Real Wages – And What It Might Take To End It', *National Institute Economic Review* 228, R3–16.

17. https://d2ufo47lrtsv5s.cloudfront.net/content/early/2017/04/25/science.aan3264.full.

18. https://www.minneapolisfed.org/publications/the-region/interview-with-lawrence-katz.

19. https://en.wikipedia.org/wiki/Margaret_Thatcher.

20. https://en.wikipedia.org/wiki/Adele.

21. https://www.nobelprize.org/nobel_prizes/chemistry/laureates/1996/kroto-bio.html.

22. https://www.theguardian.com/film/2006/oct/15/comedy.drama.

23. A. Eyles and S. Machin (2015), 'The Introduction of Academy Schools to England's Education', Centre for Economic Performance, London School of Economics, Discussion Paper 1368.

24. A. Abdulkadiroglu *et al.* (2011), 'Accountability and Flexibility in Public Schools: Evidence from Boston's charters and pilots', *Quarterly Journal of Economics* 126, 699–748; R. Fryer (2014), 'Injecting Charter School Best Practices into Traditional Public Schools: Evidence from field experiments, *Quarterly Journal of Economics* 129, 1355–1407.

25. D. D. Goldhader , D. J. Brewer and D. J. Anderson (1999) 'A Three-way Error Components Analysis of Educational Productivity', Education Economics 7:3; http://www.tandfonline.com/doi/abs/10.1080/09645299900000018.

26. https://educationendowmentfoundation.org.uk/our-work/projects/promising/.

27. Sutton Trust (2013), 'NFER Polling of Teachers'; https://www.suttontrust.com/newsarchive/nfer-poll-results-teachers-spending-pupil-premium/.

28. http://ftp.iza.org/dp2204.pdf. Note: If the world is more equal, then education can prove its worth. Just one social mobility study has demonstrated an impact from education reform. The creation of comprehensive schools in Finland during the 1970s reduced the country's intergenerational income correlation, or beta, by several percentage points.

29. London's education turnaround prompted one education leader to proclaim: 'There's a potential model here for a more equal, socially mobile society.' http://www.telegraph.co.uk/education/educationopinion/10475000/London-schools-are-a-UK-education-success-story.html.

30. http://www.centreforlondon.org/wp-content/uploads/2016/08/Lessons-from-London-Schools.pdf.

31. https://www.gov.uk/government/uploads/system/uploads/attachment_data/file/184093/DFE-RR215.pdf.

32. J. Blanden *et al.* (2015), 'Understanding the Improved Performance of Disadvantaged Pupils in London', Social Policy in a Cold Climate Discussion Paper 21; http://sticerd.lse.ac.uk/dps/case/spcc/wp21.pdf.

33. S. Burgess (2014), 'Understanding the Success of London's Schools' Centre for Markets and Public Organisation, Working Paper 14/333; http://

www.bristol.ac.uk/media-library/sites/cmpo/migrated/documents/wp333.pdf.

34. https://www.theguardian.com/commentisfree/2014/nov/14/london-schools-immigration-children-education.

35. By 2015/16 average family income in the capital was just under £1,000 a week, around twice the national average.

36. B. Bell, J. Blundell and S. Machin (2017), 'Mind the Gap: The role of demographics in explaining the "London effect"', Centre for Economic Performance, London School of Economics, unpublished paper.

37. Source for figures 7.1 and 7.2: own calculations from Labour Force Survey and Households Below Average Income data.

38. https://www.gov.uk/government/uploads/system/uploads/attachment_data/file/347915/Elitist_Britain_-_Final.pdf.

39. Young coined the term 'meritocracy', a term adopted in a positive light by Tony Blair and subsequent leaders, much to Young's chagrin. See http://www.guardian.co.uk/politics/2001/jun/29/comment.

40. http://news.bbc.co.uk/1/hi/uk_politics/3732184.stm.

41. 'Britain, the Great Meritocracy': Prime Minister's speech, 9 September 2016; https://www.gov.uk/government/speeches/britain-the-great-meritocracy-prime-ministers-speech.

42. https://en.wikipedia.org/wiki/List_of_University_of_Oxford_people_with_PPE_degrees; https://www.theguardian.com/education/2017/feb/23/ppe-oxford-university-degree-that-rules-britain.

43. http://www.theguardian.com/media/2006/jun/19/mondaymediasection2.

44. L. MacMillan (2010), 'Social Mobility and the Professions', submission to the Panel for Fair Access to the Professions; http://www.bris.ac.uk/cmpo/publications/other/socialmobility.pdf.

45. http://www.independent.co.uk/news/uk/crime/judges-are-out-of-touch-says-furious-blunkett-104765.html.

46. http://www.telegraph.co.uk/news/uknews/law-and-order/9976400/Judges-lead-sheltered-lives-warns-Britains-most-senior-female-judge.html.

47. https://hbr.org/2017/03/teams-solve-problems-faster-when-theyre-more-cognitively-diverse.

48. K. Steven, J. Dowell, C. Jackson and B. Guthriw (2011), 'Fair Access to Medicine? Retrospective analysis of UK medical schools application data 2009–2012 using three measures of socioeconomic status', BMC *Medical Education* 16, 11.

49. https://www.graham-center.org/dam/rgc/documents/publications-reports/monographs-books/Specialty-geography-compressed.pdf.

50. http://www.dailymail.co.uk/wires/pa/article-3869720/Support-drama-schools-working-class-actors-says-Michael-Sheen.html.

51. https://www.instituteforgovernment.org.uk/sites/default/files/publications/IfG_All_change_report_FINAL.pdf.

52. https://www.instituteforgovernment.org.uk/sites/default/files/publications/IfG_All_change_report_FINAL.pdf. Incidentally it was Wolf's mother Alison whose review found that nearly half of all students in England had failed to achieve a C grade in GCSE in English or maths by age 16.

CHAPTER 8: RETHINKING WORK AND EDUCATION – IMPROVING ABSOLUTE MOBILITY

1. G. Esping-Andersen (1990), *Three Worlds of Welfare Capitalism*, Princeton University Press. J. Goldthorpe (1984), 'The End of Convergence: Corporatist and dualist tendencies in modern western societies' in J. Goldthorpe (ed.), *Order and Conflict in Contemporary Capitalism: Studies in the political economy of western European nations*, Clarendon Press; J. Goldthorpe and C. Mills (2004), 'Trends in Intergenerational Class Mobility in Britain in the Late Twentieth Century' in R. Breen (ed.), *Social Mobility in Europe*, Oxford University Press.

2. M. Amior and A. Manning (2015), 'The Persistence of Local Joblessness', Centre for Economic Performance, London School of Economics, Discussion Paper 1357.

3. Ruth Davidson, (2017), 'Ctrl + Alt + Del: Conservatives must reboot capitalism', UnHerd; https://unherd.com/2017/07/ctrl-alt-del-conservatives-must-reboot-capitalism/.

4. Sutton Trust (2014), 'Evaluation of the Impact of the Sutton Trust's University Access Summer School Programme'; https://www.suttontrust.com/wp-content/uploads/2014/08/summer-school-summary-final-draft.pdf.

5. http://www.bbc.com/news/education-37011068.

6. https://www.theguardian.com/business/2016/jul/22/mike-ashley-running-sports-direct-like-victorian-workhouse.

7. http://www.pewinternet.org/2017/05/03/the-future-of-jobs-and-jobs-training/.

8. http://webarchive.nationalarchives.gov.uk/+/http:/www.culture.gov.uk/images/publications/CEPFeb2008.pdf.

9. OECD (2016), 'Building Skills for All: A review of England'; https://www.oecd.org/unitedkingdom/building-skills-for-all-review-of-england.pdf.

10. http://www.bbc.co.uk/careers/trainee-schemes-and-apprenticeships.

11. P. Hall and D. Soskice (2001), *Varieties of Capitalism: The institutional foundations of comparative advantage*, Oxford University Press.

12. The 2017 LSE Growth Commission makes this precise point, http://www.lse.ac.uk/researchAndExpertise/units/growthCommission/documents/pdf/2017LSEGCReport.pdf.

13. https://www.ons.gov.uk/employmentandlabourmarket/peopleinwork/earningsandworkinghours/bulletins/annualsurveyofhoursandearnings/2016provisionalresults.

14. From ONS, these are the real (i.e., price adjusted) growth in output per hour (GVA deflator) and Annual Survey of Hours and Earnings weekly earnings (CPIH deflator).

15. They have been referred to as such in the work on low labour shares in US companies like Apple, Facebook and Google: see D. Autor *et al.* (2017), 'Concentrating on the Fall of the Labor Share', *American Economic Review*, Papers and Proceedings 107, 180–85.

16. https://www.tes.com/news/school-news/breaking-views/after-sitting-28-gcse-papers-four-weeks-i-was-left-thinking-what-was.

17. A student's grade is a relative score masquerading as absolute one – the flaw in assessment is as true now as it was in 1970 – https://www.rand.org/content/dam/rand/pubs/reports/2008/R488.pdf.

18. http://feweek.co.uk/2017/08/24/tens-of-thousands-more-students-will-need-to-resit-english-gcses/.

19. E. Bukodi, R. Erikson and J. H. Goldthorpe (2013), 'The Effects of Social Origins and Cognitive Ability on Educational Attainment: Evidence from Britain and Sweden', Oxford University, Barnett Papers in Social Research, Working Paper 13-04; http://d307gmaoxpdmsg.cloudfront.net/BarnettPaper.pdf. See also F. Galindo-Rueda and A. Vignoles (2005), 'The Declining Relative Importance of Ability in Predicting Educational Attainment', *Journal of Human Resources* 40, 335–53.

20. OECD (2015), 'Programme for International Student Assessment (PISA): Results from PISA 2015'; https://www.oecd.org/pisa/PISA-2015-United-Kingdom.pdf.

21. OECD (2016), 'Building Skills for All: A review of England'; https://www.oecd.org/unitedkingdom/building-skills-for-all-review-of-england.pdf. In England, one-third of those aged 16–19 were found to have low basic skills. The presence of migrants in the population does not alter the overall picture.

22. Kenneth Baker (2013), *14–18: A new vision for secondary education*, Bloomsbury; https://www.bloomsbury.com/uk/ 14-18-a-new-vision-for-secondary-education-9781780938448/.

23. H. Kennedy (1997), 'Learning Works: Widening participation in further education', Further Education Funding Council; http://dera.ioe. ac.uk/15073/2/Learning%20works%20-%20widening%20participation%20 in%20further%20education%20(Kennedy%20report).pdf.

24. Paper on poor skills matching between colleges and employers.

25. A. Brown and E. Keep (1999), 'Review of Vocational Education and Training Research in the United Kingdom', report for European COST Action A11 programme on vocational education in Europe; https://www2.warwick. ac.uk/fac/soc/ier/people/abrown/publications/kina19243enc_0011.pdf.

26. https://www.ft.com/content/33044938-0de8-11e6-ad80-67655613c2d6.

27. E. Hanushek and L. Woessmann (2015), *The Knowledge Capital of Nations: Education and the economics of growth*, MIT Press.

28. James Heckman, 'Research Summary: The lifecycle benefits of an influential early childhood program'; https://heckmanequation.org/ resource/research-summary-lifecycle-benefits-influential-early-childhood-program/. Heckman's research presents estimates that every dollar invested in quality early childhood development for disadvantaged children produces a 7–10 per cent return, per child, per year – due to reduced costs in later life.

29. The Abecedarian Project, http://abc.fpg.unc.edu/; HighScope Perry Preschool Study, https://highscope.org/perrypreschoolstudy.

30. Much of the benefit comes from crime reduction in adulthood, see J. Heckman, R. Pinto and P. Savelyev (2013), 'Understanding the Mechanisms Through Which an Influential Early Childhood Program Boosted Adult Outcomes', *American Economic Review* 103, 2052–86.

31. National Evaluation of Sure Start Team (2010), 'The Impact of Sure Start Local Programmes on Five Year Olds and Their Families', Department of Education Research Report DFE-RR067; https://www.gov.uk/government/ uploads/system/uploads/attachment_data/file/182026/DFE-RR067.pdf.

32. https://www.early-education.org.uk/news/ election-statement-early-educations-president-and-vice-presidents.

33. E. Hanushek and S. Rivkin (2012), 'The Distribution of Teacher Quality and Implications for Policy', *Annual Review of Economics* 4, 131–57.

34. OECD (2011), 'Building a High-Quality Teaching Profession: Lessons from around the world'; https://www2.ed.gov/about/inits/ed/internationaled/ background.pdf.

35. R. Coe *et al.* (2014), *What Makes Great Teaching? Review of the underpinning research*, Sutton Trust; http://www.suttontrust.com/wp-content/uploads/2014/10/What-Makes-Great-Teaching-REPORT.pdf.

36. Ibid.

37. https://www.dur.ac.uk/news/research/?itemno=29978.

38. Sutton Trust (2017), 'Pupil Premium Polling'; https://www.suttontrust.com/research-paper/pupil-premium-polling-2017/.

39. The title of the film *Waiting for Superman* was inspired by Canada's tale of finding out as a crestfallen child that Superman wasn't real. As a nine-year-old, Canada had clung on to the hope that Superman would one day come to rescue him and his family. Canada's own life was transformed at the age of nine when he moved from one of New York's poorest neighbourhoods to his grandparents' home and a better school. He went on to study at the Harvard Graduate School of Education, https://en.wikipedia.org/wiki/Waiting_for_%22Superman%22; http://prospect.org/article/audacity-harlem

40. P. Tough (2017), *Whatever it Takes: Geoffrey Canada's quest to change Harlem and America*, Mariner Books.

41. W. Dobbie and R. Fryer (2011), 'Are High-Quality Schools Enough to Increase Achievement among the Poor? Evidence from the Harlem Children's Zone', *American Economic Journal: Applied* 3, 158–87.

42. Ibid. The real test of the out-of-school interventions may be long-term life outcomes of children: http://www.heritage.org/education/report/assessing-the-harlem-childrens-zone#_ftnref50.

43. http://www.nytimes.com/2010/10/13/education/13harlem.html.

44. https://www.ed.gov/news/press-releases/secretary-duncan-announces-seventeen-2012-promise-neighborhoods-winners-school-s.

45. http://harvardpolitics.com/united-states/promise-harlem-children-zone/

46. https://www.help.senate.gov/imo/media/doc/Canada.pdf. Philanthropists helped Canada build up assets of more than $200 million for the programme.

47. https://www.gov.uk/government/news/education-secretary-announces-6-new-opportunity-areas.

CHAPTER 9: UNLOCKING THE ELITES – IMPROVING RELATIVE MOBILITY

1. C. Tilly (1998), 'How to Hoard Opportunities' in C. Tilly, *Durable Inequality*, University of California Press.

2. Greg Buzwell (2014), 'An Introduction to *Jude the Obscure*', British Library website; https://www.bl.uk/romantics-and-victorians/articles/an-introduction-to-jude-the-obscure.

3. Kathryn Hughes (2014), 'The Middle Classes: Etiquette and upward mobility', British Library website; https://www.bl.uk/romantics-and-victorians/articles/the-middle-classes-etiquette-and-upward-mobility. Advice for anxious social climbers included how to deal with dirty nails or bad breath and how to style your beard. Crises of identity among those moving from one class to another are at the heart of the most memorable fiction from the period. In Charles Dickens' *Great Expectations*, Pip goes from poor blacksmith to London gentleman, but ultimately rejects the superficial affectations of gentlemanly behaviour. In *The Great Gatsby* the central character Jay Gatsby may have made all the wealth in the world, but will never be accepted into the old money social elites.

4. D. Kahneman, J. Knetsch and R. Thaler (1991), 'Anomalies: The Endowment Effect, Loss Aversion, and Status Quo Bias', *Journal of Economic Perspectives* 5, 193–206.

5. https://en.wikipedia.org/wiki/John_Hervey,_7th_Marquess_of_Bristol#Early_years_and_family.

6. https://www.theguardian.com/g2/story/0,3604,439752,00.html.

7. https://www.gov.uk/government/uploads/system/uploads/attachment_data/file/447575/Downward_mobility_opportunity_hoarding_and_the_glass_floor.pdf.

8. https://www.brookings.edu/wp-content/uploads/2016/06/glass-floor-downward-mobility-equality-opportunity-hoarding-reeves-howard.pdf.

9. R. Reeves (2017,) *Dream Hoarders*, Brookings Institution.

10. https://www.theguardian.com/inequality/2017/jul/15/how-us-middle-classes-hoard-opportunity-privilege.

11. 'Yes, I Was a Failure at School, Dad, I Blame You', *Sunday Times*, 8 February 2009; https://www.thetimes.co.uk/article/yes-i-was-a-failure-at-school-dad-i-blame-you-t67xgbgbcnp.

12. 'No More of This Cavalier Experiment', *Sunday Times*, 5 August 2012; https://www.thetimes.co.uk/article/no-more-of-this-cavalier-experiment-lfw6k35lxjl.

13. S. Aldridge (2001), 'Social Mobility: A discussion paper', Performance and Innovation Unit; http://kumlai.free.fr/RESEARCH/THESE/TEXTE/MOBILITY/mobility%20salariale/SOCIAL%20MOBILITY.pdf.

14. L. Hanley (2017), *Respectable: Crossing the class divide*, Penguin.

15. https://www.theguardian.com/books/2016/apr/17/lynsey-hanley-how-i-became-middle-class-respectable-experience-of-class-extract.

16. Lee Elliot Major, 'I Hope My Story Shows What Can Be Achieved', *Times Educational Supplement*, 11 September 2015; full version at http://www.suttontrust.com/newsarchive/i-hope-my-story-shows-what-can-be-achieved-lee-elliot-major/.

17. https://www.brookings.edu/blog/social-mobility-memos/2013/10/24/pursuing-happiness-social-mobility-and-well-being/.

18. A. Miles, M. Savage and F. Bühlmann (2011), 'Telling a Modest Story: Accounts of men's upward mobility from the National Child Development Study', *British Journal of Sociology* 62, 418–41.

19. R. Hoggart (1957), *The Uses of Literacy: Aspects of working class life*, Transaction Publishers; A. Lovell (1957), 'The Scholarship Boy', *Universities and Left Review* 1:2; http://banmarchive.org.uk/collections/ulr/2_scolarship.pdf.

20. http://www.prospectmagazine.co.uk/features/moremobilethanwethink.

21. http://www.radiotimes.com/news/2014-09-16/david-morrissey-intern-culture-could-squeeze-those-from-disadvantaged-backgrounds-out-of-acting.

22. https://www.thestage.co.uk/news/2017/mps-call-ban-unpaid-arts-internships/.

23. https://actoring.co.uk/2016/04/15/the-class-ceiling-for-british-actors/.

24. https://www.theguardian.com/business/2016/nov/04/government-refuses-to-ban-unpaid-internships.

25. http://www.dailymail.co.uk/tvshowbiz/article-2315853/Im-posh-kid-insists-toffee-named-Benedict-Cumberbatch.html.

26. http://www.telegraph.co.uk/culture/music/music-news/9955716/Pop-stars-now-are-just-puppets-on-a-string-says-Sandie-Shaw.html.

27. http://www.dailymail.co.uk/news/article-1356469/Cash-internships-Tory-backers-pay-2k-time-buy-children-work-experience.html.

28. http://www.telegraph.co.uk/news/politics/8469243/David-Cameron-reignites-intern-row.html.

29. http://www.telegraph.co.uk/news/politics/nick-clegg/8430087/Nick-Clegg-I-was-wrong-to-use-fathers-help-to-secure-bank-internship.html.

30. http://www.bbc.com/news/uk-41717401.

31. http://schoolsweek.co.uk/school-admissions-secrets-lies-and-local-authorities/.

32. One suggestion might be to allocate half of places at a school to the children living close by and use a ballot for the remaining half. See http://www.suttontrust.com/researcharchive/selective-comprehensives-2017/.

33. https://twitter.com/PCollinsTimes/status/774197199446151168.

34. Sutton Trust (2014), 'Ballots and Banding'; https://www.suttontrust.com/research-paper/ballots-banding/.

35. Sutton Trust (2014), 'Survey of Parents'; http://www.suttontrust.com/newsarchive/lotteries-should-decide-secondary-school-admissions-parents-say/.

36. Sutton Trust (2016), 'Leading People 2016'; http://www.suttontrust.com/wp-content/uploads/2016/02/Leading-People_Feb16.pdf.

37. S. Burgess, M. Dickson and L. Macmillan (2014), 'Selective Schooling Systems Increase Inequality', Institute of Education Department of Quantitative Social Science, Working Paper 14-09; http://repec.ioe.ac.uk/REPEc/pdf/qsswp1409.pdf.

38. In the 1960s selective state schools taught around 25 per cent of state pupils – those who passed the eleven plus (an academic test sat at age 11); when in 1965 the Education Secretary Anthony Crosland issued his edict calling on local authorities to abolish selection, there were over 1,000 grammar schools in England and Wales. See http://www.suttontrust.com/wp-content/uploads/2008/10/SuttonTrustFullReportFinal.pdf.

39. Sutton Trust (2013), 'Poor Grammar'; http://www.suttontrust.com/researcharchive/poor-grammar-entry-grammar-schools-disadvantaged-pupils-england/.

40. http://theconversation.com/grammar-schools-why-academic-selection-only-benefits-the-very-affluent-74189.

41. Sutton Trust (2012), 'Open Access: Democratising entry to independent day schools'; http://www.suttontrust.com/wp-content/uploads/2014/08/open-access-report-march-2012-final-2.pdf. Peter Lampl, the son of Viennese immigrants who escaped the Nazis in the Second World War, founded the Sutton Trust charity that has helped tens of thousands of state school students to access the world's most prestigious universities in Britain and the United States.

42. Sutton Trust (2014), 'Belvedere Evaluation'; http://www.suttontrust.com/wp-content/uploads/2014/08/BelvedereEval1.pdf.

43. http://www.telegraph.co.uk/education/educationopinion/11254850/Open-top-independent-schools-to-all-on-merit.html.

44. Sutton Trust (2015), 'Open Access: Update'; http://www.suttontrust.com/wp-content/uploads/2012/03/Open-Access-Report-March-2015-UPDATE.pdf.

45. http://researchbriefings.parliament.uk/ResearchBriefing/Summary/SN05222. Private schools argue that they already open up their facilities to

state schools. The children they educate relieve the pressure on an already overstretched state school system.

46. 'What If There Was a College-Admissions Lottery?', *Atlantic*, 14 May 2014; http://www.theatlantic.com/education/archive/2014/05/the-case-for-a-college-admissions-lottery/361585/. A similar argument has been put forward for the highly competitive admissions in Ivy League universities in the United States. They too are bombarded by thousands of indistinguishable super-smart candidates. The reality is admissions officers are already making random decisions about who to enrol.

47. A. Zimdars, A. Sullivan and A. Heath (2009), 'Elite Higher Education Admissions in the Arts and Sciences: Is cultural capital the key?', *Sociology* 43, 648–66.

48. S. Lucieer, K. Stegers-Jager, M. R. Rikers and A. Themmen (2016), 'Non-Cognitive Selected Students Do Not Outperform Lottery-Admitted Students in the Pre-Clinical Stage of Medical School', *Advances in Health Science Education* 21, 51–61.

49. Sutton Trust (2009), 'Innovative Admissions'; http://www.suttontrust. com/wp-content/uploads/2009/07/innovativeadmissions09.pdf. Some universities are reserving extra university places for a pre-degree preparatory year for disadvantaged students over and above core degree places. The admitted students have fared extremely well in their subsequent degrees. This is an approach that increases absolute mobility; more education opportunities are created, but not at the expense of others.

50. R. Murphy and F. Weinhardt (2014), 'Top of the Class: The importance of ordinal rank', Centre for Economic Performance, London School of Economics, Discussion Paper 1241; B. Elsner and I. Isphording (2015), 'Big Fishes in Small Ponds: Ability rank and human capital investment', IZA Discussion Paper 9121.

51. 'Why Public Schools Still Feed Oxbridge', *New Statesman*, May 2007; http://www.newstatesman.com/society/2007/09/fee-charging-schools-oxbridge.

52. G. Solon (2017), 'What Do We Know So Far about Multigenerational Mobility?', National Bureau of Economic Research, Working Paper 21053.

53. http://www.oxfordreference.com/view/10.1093/oi/authority. 20110803095618608.

54. https://en.wiktionary.org/wiki/clogs_to_clogs_in_three_generations.

55. G. Becker and N. Tomes (1986), 'On Human Capital and the Rise and Fall of Families', *Journal of Labor Economics* 4, S1–S39.

56. G. Clark (2014), *The Son Also Rises: Surnames and the history of social mobility*, Princeton University Press.

57. The surnames include Berkeley, Baskerville, Darcy, Mandeville, Montgomery, Neville, Pakenham, Percy, Punchard and Talbot.

58. Cameron is a Scottish surname and relatively common throughout the English-speaking world.

59. http://www.historyofparliamentonline.org/volume/1604-1629/member/sawyer-edmund-15867-1676.

60. https://en.wikipedia.org/wiki/Family_of_David_Cameron. Cameron's father, grandfather and great-grandfather were all successful financiers. Cameron's maternal grandfather meanwhile was the British Army officer Sir William Mount.

61. https://www.theguardian.com/commentisfree/2015/feb/04/social-mobility-equality-class-society.

62. https://www.economist.com/news/books-and-arts/21595396-new-study-shows-just-how-slow-it-change-social-class-have-and-have-not.

63. P. Saunders (2010), *Social Mobility Myths*, Civitas.

64. D. Hambrick *et al.* (2016), 'Chapter One – Beyond Born versus Made: A new look at expertise', *Psychology of Learning and Motivation* 64, 1–55.

65. R. Plomin and I. Deary (2015), 'Genetics and Intelligence Differences: Five special findings', *Molecular Psychiatry* 20, 98–108.

66. Miles Corak (2014), 'Economics for Public Policy'; https://milescorak.com/2014/05/22/social-mobility-fixed-forever-gregory-clarks-the-son-also-rises-is-a-book-of-scholarship-and-of-scholastic-overreach/.

67. Solon (2017).

68. Ibid.

69. OECD (2018), ' A Broken Social Elevator?' http://oe.cd/social-mobility-2018.

70. The Sutton Trust, for example, has supported 25,000 young people from low- and middle-income backgrounds, many of whom have graduated at the country's most prestigious universities.

71. http://www.telegraph.co.uk/education/2017/09/05/state-schools-students-likely-become-high-flying-doctors-used/.

72. http://all-that-is-interesting.com/lineage-british-royal-family.

73. http://uk.businessinsider.com/sunday-times-rich-list-2016-the-aristocrats-that-are-richer-than-the-queen-2017-1/#1-hugh-grosvenor-son-of-the-recently-deceased-duke-of-westminster-14.

74. http://www.telegraph.co.uk/news/society/11383148/Why-the-aristocracy-always-win.html.

75. T. Chan and V. Boliver (2013), 'The Grandparents Effect in Social Mobility: Evidence from British birth cohort studies', *American Sociological Review* 78, 662–78.

76. https://www.bl.uk/collection-items/letter-from-charles-dickens-on-ragged-schools-from-the-daily-news.

77. In typically vivid detail, Dickens described a classroom scene between a teacher 'who refreshed himself by spitting every half-minute' and his pupils – a 'dull young man' a 'sharp boy', and a 'reckless guesser'. The visit had a lasting impact on his imagination: it was used as the site for Fagin's den of child pickpockets in the novel *Oliver Twist*. It is said to have influenced *A Christmas Carol*, inspiring the book's themes of poverty and education. Many characters in Dickens' novels make transitions between the social classes, moving from poverty into wealth in Victorian Britain. *David Copperfield* is a tale of upward mobility. Pip goes from blacksmith to gentleman in *Great Expectations*. Dickens' letters can now be found at the British Library near King's Cross Station – a stone's throw away from the ragged school he visited. See https://www.bl.uk/romantics-and-victorians/articles/great-expectations-and-class, https://www.bl.uk/collection-items/letter-from-charles-dickens-on-ragged-schools-from-the-daily-news.

Index

90:10 earnings ratio, 8, 9, 49

A

absolute mobility, 16, 41, 51–5, 159–60
academy schools, 122, 123, 162–3
accents, and social class, 15
acting industry:
– and internships, 203
– and private education, 137, 138, 140, 171
Adele (singer), 162
Allen, Lily, 134
Alphabet (Google) company, 183
Amazon (company), 183
American dream, 31–4, 69–70, 76–7
apprenticeship system, 56, 107–8, 180–1
Association of University Teachers, 95
Atkinson, Rowan, 134
Attlee, Clement, 139
Austen, Jane, 41
Australia, 29–31, 180
automation, 56–7, 178–9

B

Baker, Kenneth, 186
Baltimore, US, 63
Balzac, Honoré de, 41
Barker, Ronnie, 13
basic skills:
– gaps, 124–8
– surveys, 115–20
Bazalgette, Joseph, 212
Bazalgette, Peter, 203, 212

BBC, and apprenticeships, 181
Becker, Gary, 211
Beckham, David:
– background and meteoric rise, 3–4
– and education, 11–12
– elite position of, 18
– exceptional status of, 5, 15–16, 213
– global brand of, 8
– refused knighthood, 10
– and social class, 14–15, 196
Beckham, Victoria, 15, 18
Belvedere School, Liverpool, 208
Bennett, Alan, *The History Boys*, 162
Blackburn, Tony, 134
Blair, Tony, 122, 139, 169, 200
Branson, Richard, 137, 155
Brexit, 71–6
Bristol, Frederick Hervey, Marquess of, 197
BRIT schools, 162
Britain:
– basic skills surveys, 115–17, 118
– economic divide, 153–4
– and income mobility, 8, 10, 25–7, 29–33, 45
– post-war era, 45–7, 218
– seaside towns, 70 *see also* education system
– England
British Cohort Study (1970), 5, 7
British Museum, 203
Brown, Gordon, 160
Bullingdon Club, Oxford University, 145
Burgess, Simon, 165

C

Cabinet members, privately educated, 139
Caine, Michael, 202
Cameron, David:
– ancestry, 212–13
– background and social position, 3–4, 8, 14
– Eton education of, 11, 132–3
– and internships, 204
– on school admission by lottery, 205
– on social mobility, 18–19
– and tax avoidance, 10
– Witney constituency, 67
Cameron, Samantha, 11
Canada, 27, 29–31, 33, 117, 180
Canada, Geoffrey, 190–1
Canaletto, 131
Carey, Tanith, 83–4
Carolina Abecedarian Project (USA), 188–9
Charles I, King, 212
Charterhouse, 134
Chetty, Raj, 31, 61–2, 65–6, 68, 70, 156, 215
child development, 156–7
Chua, Amy, 84
Church, Charlotte, 134
civil service, and private education, 140
Clarendon Schools, 133, 139
Clark, Gregory, The Son Also Rises, 211–14
Clarkson, Jeremy, 134
'Class sketch,' on David Frost show, 12–13
Cleese, John, 13
Clegg, Nick, 204
Cleland, Jen, 216
Coalition Government (2010–2015), 123
Collins, Phillip, 205
Cook, Alastair, 134
Corak, Miles, 35, 37, 158, 214
Corbett, Ronnie, 13
Coren, Giles, 90–1
Cowell, Simon, 137
creative industries, 202–3
cultural capital, 14, 110–11, 144–5
Cumberbatch, Benedict, 133, 203

D

David Frost (TV show), 'Class sketch,' 12–13
Davies, Ray, 46
Davison, Ruth, 178
Day-Lewis, Daniel, 134
Denmark, 27, 29
Dickens, Charles, 217–18
Dimbleby, David, 134
Dimbleby, Jonathan, 134
divorce, and inheritance, 217
downward mobility, 54–5, 197
Dulwich College, 134
Durand Academy, Stockwell, 120–1

E

economic capital, 14
economic cost:
– of basic skills gaps, 127–8
– of low social mobility, 57–8
economic growth, effects of, 159–61
Education Endowment Foundation (EEF), 123, 164
Education Reform Act (1988), 122
education system:
– and academic testing, 184–6
– academies, 122, 123
– attempts at reform, 121–8
– grammar schools, 206–7
– inequalities of, 30, 87–9, 101
– league tables, 122
– London Challenge, 122, 165–6
– 'London effect,' 165
– national curriculum, 122, 123
– 'Pupil Premium' funds, 123
– realistic expectations of, 161–6
– school admissions, 89–91, 204–5
– selective schools, 206–8
– vocational education, 187–8
– workplace learning, 180–1
– Youth Training Scheme (YTS), 11
  see also further education
– higher education
– postgraduate education
– private education

elites, unrepresentative, 166–73
England:
– mapping mobility in, 66–8.
  See also Britain
Eno, Brian, 134
Eton College:
– and Britain's elites, 3, 11, 131–3, 134,
  139, 148
– Canaletto's painting of, 131
– fees, 146
– investigation over exam corruption, 111
– and life skills, 145
– and Oxbridge, 141
European Union, and Brexit, 71–6

F

Facebook (company), 183
family income inequality, 49
family stability, and social mobility,
  68–9
fees, university, 105–6
Feinstein, Leon, 92–4
financial capital, 144–5
financial elites, 155, 196–7
financial services industry, and private
  education, 140
Finland, 27, 120, 164, 186
Fitzgerald, F. Scott, The Great Gatsby,
  34, 35, 41
Fukuyama, Francis, 63–4
further education, 172, 187

G

genetic inheritance, and social mobility,
  213–14
Gibb, Nick, 112
'gig economy,' 56
Gini coefficients, 35, 36, 58, 68
global financial crisis (2007–8), 51
globalization, 56
Globe, The (theatre), 203
Goldthorpe, John, 88, 102, 202
Goodhart, David, 27
Gove, Michael, 120–1, 132
graduate earnings, 104, 158

grammar schools, 127, 184, 206–7
Great British Class Survey
  (BBC, 2011), 13–14
Great Gatsby Curve, 34–8, 58, 68, 156

H

Hale, Baroness, 170
Hanley, Lynsey, Respectable, 200
Hardy, Thomas, Jude the Obscure, 196
Harlem Children's Zone (HCZ),
  New York, 190–1
Harrow School, 134
Heckman, James, 188
Henman, Tim, 134
Henry VI, King, 131
higher education:
– admissions criteria, 106–7, 209–10
– and basic skills, 120
– expansion of, 95–7
– fees, 105–6
– types of degrees, 104–5 see also
  postgraduate education
Hills Road sixth-form college, 141
Hoggart, Richard, The Uses of
  Literacy, 201
home ownership, 39–41, 55–6
honours system, 15, 138
House of Lords, 136
house prices, and education,
  89–90
Hoy, Chris, 134
human capital, 144–5, 157

I

IGE (intergenerational elasticity), 25,
  27–9, 35
imposter syndrome, 200
income inequality, defence of, 154
industrial decline, 178
inheritance tax, 158–9
intergenerational income persistence,
  4, 26, 147, 164, 214–15
internships, 108, 203–4
Irons, Jeremy, 134
Izzard, Eddie, 137

J

Japan, 186
Johnson, Boris, 133, 154, 213
Johnson, Jo, 155

K

Katz, Lawrence, 72, 160, 161
Kennedy, Helena, 187
King Solomon Academy, 163
Kinks, The (band), 46
Kinnock, Neil, 215
Kinnock, Stephen, 215
Knowsley, Merseyside, 67–8, 73
Kroto, Sir Harry, 162
Krueger, Alan, 34–5, 37, 41, 68, 160

L

Labour Force Survey, 102, 108
labour market inequality, 101
Lampl, Sir Peter, 207–8
Lampson, Frank, 137
Laurie, Hugh, 134
Law, Jude, 137
legal profession, and private education,
    137–8, 170–1
lifeskills, 109–11
London:
 – declining mobility in, 77
 – and education, 122, 163, 165–6
London School of Economics (LSE), 104
 – report on income mobility (2005), 25–6, 37
lotteries: for school places, 204–5
 – for university admissions, 210

M

Macmillan, Harold, 45, 95
Major, John, 136
Manchester United Football Club, 11
Marlborough College, 11, 134
Martin, Chris, 137
May, Theresa, 76, 139, 169
Members of Parliament, privately
    educated, 138–9

meritocracy, 169
Milburn, Alan, 72
Miliband, Ed, 67
Miller, Jonathan, 199
Miller, Sienna, 137
Miller, William, 199
Mirren, Helen, 202
Morrissey, David, 202
Mossbourne Community
    Academy, 163
Mount, Harry, 216–17
Moving to Opportunity (MTO)
    experiment, 65–6, 156
music industry, 137, 180, 203

N

National Audit Office, 128
National Child Development Study
    (1958), 5, 6
national curriculum, 122, 123
National Gallery, London, 131, 148
NEETs (young people not in education,
    employment and training), 122–3
Netherlands, The, 120, 186
New York, 63, 65, 191
news journalism, and private education,
    138, 139, 170
Norway, 27

O

OECD (Organization for Economic
    Co-operation and Development):
 – basic skills surveys, 115–17, 120
 – education and training in the
    workplace, 180
 – income mobility league table, 27
Olympics, London (2012), 136
Open Access schemes, 208
Opportunity Areas, 192
'opportunity hoarders,' 195–9
Orwell, George, 132
Oscars awards, 137, 138
Oxbridge:
 – admissions criteria, 106, 196
 – and graduate earnings, 104

– and private education, 141–2, 145
– and private tutoring, 88
Oxford University, 3, 86, 145,
  162, 170

P

Paxman, Jeremy, 134
Pepys, Samuel, 212
Perry Preschool Project (USA), 188–9
PIACC (Programme for the International
  Assesment of Adult Competencies), 115,
  117, 118–19, 126
Piketty, Thomas, *Capital in the Twenty-First
  Century*, 10–11, 41
postgraduate education, 100–1
'precariat' 14, 56
private education:
– academic benefits of, 140–4
– and Britain's elites, 134–40
– charitable status of schools, 208
– Eton College, 131–3
– exclusivity of, 207–8
– fees, 145–7
– non-academic benefits of, 144–5
– threat to social mobility, 147–8
– wage differentials, 144
private tuition, 84–6
productivity puzzle, 51, 56–7
Promise Academies (USA), 191
'Promise Neighborhood' (USA),
  191–2
public service workers, 182
publishing, and private education, 140
'Pupil Premium' funds, 123
Putnam, Robert, 69

R

recessions, 1980s, 47
Redmayne, Eddie, 133
Reeves, Richard,
  Dream Hoarders, 198
relative mobility, 16–17
riots, England (2011), 120, 128
Robbins, Lord Lionel, 95–7
Royal family, 216

'rug rat race,' 92
Rugby School, 134

S

Saez, Emmanuel, 61
San Jose, California, 76–7
Sawyer, Sir Edmund, 212
schools. *See* education system
Sex Pistols, 46
Shaw, Sandie, 203
Sheen, Michael, 171
social capital, 14, 69, 109–10, 144–5
social class hierarchies, 12–15
social diversity, among elites, 166–73
Social Mobility Commission, 136, 169
Social Mobility Index, 66–8
social welfare, 156
socio-economic status (SES), 92
soft skills, 110, 144–5
Solon, Gary, 214–15
South Korea, 186
St Paul's Boys' School, 134, 141, 199
St Paul's Girls' School, 141
'stagflation,' 46
statistics, 61–2
Stiglitz, Joseph, 58
Sunday Times Rich List, 136
Sure Start centres, 189
surnames, research on, 211–13, 216
Sutton Trust, 25, 66, 123, 134, 141

T

Tawney, R. H., *Equality*, 159
tax avoidance, 10
tax data, 61–2
tax system, 155, 158–9
teachers, importance of, 189–90
technology companies, 183
teenage mothers, 30, 68
teenagers, low-skilled, 186
Thatcher, Margaret, 154, 161
'tiger mums,' 83–4
Tilly, Charles, *Durable Inequality*, 195
Tomes, Nigel, 211
Toynbee, Polly, 92

trade unions, 56, 181
training, in the workplace, 180–1
'trickle-down economics,' 47–9
Trump, Donald, 71–2, 76

U

United State of America:
– and the American Dream, 33–4, 42, 69–70, 76–7
– basic skills surveys, 117
– charter schools, 163
– mapping mobility in, 61–6, 68–70
university admissions, 104–8, 209–10
  see also higher education

V

vocational education, 172, 187–8

W

wages, stagnant and falling, 182–3
Walters, Julie, 202
wealth inequality, 10–11, 16–17, 39
Weller, Paul, 132–3
Wellington, Duke of, 132
Wellington College, 134

West, Dominic, 63
Westminster School, 134, 141
Wilby, Peter, 89, 210
Wilkinson, Jonny, 134
William IV, King, 212
Willoughby, Holly, 137
Wilshaw, Michael, 71
Winchester College, 134
Winslet, Kate, 134
Wire, The (TV series), 63
Wolf, Alison/ Wolf review, 124
Wolf, Rachel, 172
workplace training, 180–1

X

X Factor, The (TV show), 203

Y

Young, Cristobel, 155
Young, Michael, *The Rise of the Meritocracy*, 147, 169, 183–4
Youth Training Scheme (YTS), 11

Z

Zeta-Jones, Catherine, 137